Prophecy Checklist

From the Apostasy to the Final Judgment

To Dany —

Norma Pyper Mitchell

Prophecy Checklist

From the Apostasy to the Final Judgment

Compiled by

Norma Pyper Mitchell

BONNEVILLE BOOKS ™
Springville, Utah

ISBN: 1-55517-559-7
v.1
Published by Bonneville Books
Imprint of Cedar Fort Inc.
925 N. Main Springville, Ut., 84663
www.cedarfort.com

Distributed by:

Typeset by Virginia Reeder
Cover design by Adam Ford
Cover design © 2001 by Lyle Mortimer

Printed in the United States of America
10 9 8 7 6 5 4 3 2 1
Printed on acid-free paper

Library of Congress Cataloging-in-Publication Data

> Prophecy checklist : from the apostasy to the final judgment /
> compiled by Norma Pyper Mitchell.
> p. cm.
> Includes bibliographical references.
> ISBN 1-55517-559-7 (pbk. : alk. paper)
> 1. Bible--Prophecies. 2. Bible--Prophecies--Chronology. I. Mitchell,
> Norma Pyper.
> BS647.2 .P74 2001
> 231.7'45'088283--dc21
>   2001003642

iv

PROPHECY CHECKLIST

Which prophecies have been fulfilled?
What must take place before the Second Coming?

❑ We cannot endure on borrowed light
❑ Persecution follows financial bondage
❑ Nations of the earth against the Kingdom of God
❑ Stand in holy places

❑ The western boundary of Missouri to be swept clean
❑ A leader like unto Moses
❑ A command to return
❑ The City of Zion (the new Jerusalem)
❑ The plan
❑ Under the direction of the Lord
❑ To be built by a remnant of Jacob assisted by the Gentiles
❑ A land of peace
❑ A temple will be built
❑ Jesus will appear
❑ Freedom of religion

❑ Who is Israel?
❑ The fate of Judah
❑ The Lost Tribes taken by the Assyrians
❑ Many mixed with the people where they were scattered
❑ The main body departed to the north
❑ Zion will be established before their return
❑ Prophets of the Lost Tribes
❑ A history to be kept
❑ Preparation for their return
❑ An inheritance in Palestine

KEY TO ABBREVIATIONS

CN	*Church News*
CR	Conference Report
D&C	Doctrine and Covenants
DEN	*Deseret Evening News*
DHC	Documentary History of the Church
HC	*History of the Church*
DN	*Deseret News*
IE	*Improvement Era*
JD	*Journal of Discourses*
JI	*Juvenile Instructor*
MS	*Millennial Star*
JS	Joseph Smith translation

QUOTES FROM GENERAL AUTHORITIES

Ballard, Melvin J.	Apostle	Pratt, Parley P.	Apostle
Benson, Ezra Taft	Prophet	Pratt, Orson	Apostle
Cannon, George Q.	Apostle	Smith, Joseph Jr.	Prophet
Clark, Reuben J.	Apostle	Smith, Joseph Fielding	Prophet
Hyde, Orson	Apostle	Snow, Erastus	Apostle
Kimball, Heber C.	Apostle	Talmage, James E.	Apostle
Kimball, Spencer W.	Prophet	Taylor, John	Prophet
Lee, Harold B.	Prophet	Whitney, Orson F.	Apostle
McConkie, Bruce R.	Apostle	Wirthlin, Joseph L.	Apostle
McKay, David O.	Prophet	Woodruff, Wilford	Prophet
Morris, George Q.	Apostle	Young, Brigham	Prophet
Penrose, Charles W.	Apostle		

INTRODUCTION

"And it shall come to pass that he that feareth me shall be looking forth for the great day of the Lord to come, even for the signs of the coming of the Son of Man." D&C 45:39.

Several books have been written concerning prophecy and the last days. This book differs from others. It provides scriptures and the words of prophets and general authorities rather than personal opinions and commentaries. The main signs we can expect as prophecy unfolds are presented in a checklist form so that (1) prophecies that have been or are presently being fulfilled may be identified, and (2) those that are still to come will be recognized.

Most of the prophecies included in these pages will be familiar to Latter-day Saints, but the original sources are unknown to the average person. My intent has been to bring the prophecies together in one book so that the reader will have immediate access to not only an overview of our destiny but the source of the knowledge the Lord has given. A few prophecies quoted by some Latter-day Saints have not been included in this collection. My research proved their sources to be questionable.

Each prophecy has been given a number. The numbered sections following the checklist provide scriptures and quotes for individual prophecies. Not every quote available has been included. It is hoped that the reader will study the scriptures and the words of the prophets to gain further understanding of the Lord's plans.

The prophecies may not be fulfilled in the order they have been placed in this book. Some will probably overlap. With information and understanding, we can prepare for the second coming of Jesus Christ. What an exciting time to be alive and witness the last days before the coming of our Savior in all His glory.

"And take heed to yourselves, lest at any time your hearts be overcharged with surfeiting [debauchery, rioting and reveling], and drunkeness, and cares [worldliness] of this life, and so that day come upon you unawares. For as a snare shall it come on all them that dwell on the face of the whole earth. Watch ye therefore, and pray always, that ye may be accounted worthy to escape all these things that shall come to pass, and to stand before the Son of man" (Luke 21:34–36).

—1—

❏ JESUS CHRIST ESTABLISHED HIS CHURCH

And he goeth up into a mountain, and calleth unto him whom he would: and they came unto him.

And he ordained twelve, that they should be with him, and that he might send them forth to preach,

And to have power to heal sicknesses, and to cast out devils (Mark 3:13–15).

Think not that I am come to send peace on earth: I came not to send peace, but a sword. . . .

And he that taketh not his cross, and followeth after me, is not worthy of me.

He that findeth his life shall lose it: and he that loseth his life for my sake shall find it (Matthew 10:34,38–39).

Afterward he appeared unto the eleven as they sat at meat, and upbraided them with their unbelief and hardness of heart, because they believed not them which had seen him after he was risen.

And he said unto them, Go ye into all the world, and preach the gospel to every creature.

He that believeth and is baptized shall be saved; but he that believeth not shall be damned.

And these signs shall follow them that believe; In my

name shall they cast out devils; they shall speak with new tongues;

They shall take up serpents; and if they drink any deadly thing, it shall not hurt them; they shall lay hands on the sick, and they shall recover.

So then after the Lord had spoken unto them, he was received up into heaven, and sat on the right hand of God.

And they went forth, and preached everywhere, the Lord working with them, and confirming the word with signs following (Mark 16:14–20).

After these things the Lord appointed other seventy also, and sent them two and two before his face into every city and place, whither he himself would come.

Therefore said he unto them, The harvest truly is great, but the labourers are few: Pray ye therefore the Lord of the harvest, that he would send forth labourers into his harvest (Luke 10:1–2).

And they gave forth their lots; and the lot fell upon Matthias; and he was numbered with the eleven apostles (Acts 1:26).

Thus, then, under a celestial influence and co-operation, the doctrine of the Savior, like the rays of the sun, quickly irradiated the whole world. Presently, in accordance with divine prophecy, the sound of His inspired evangelists and apostles had gone throughout all the earth, and their words to the ends of the world. Throughout every city and village, like a replenished barn floor, churches were rapidly abounding and filled with members from every people. Those who, in consequence of the delusions that had descended to them from their ancestors, had been fettered by the ancient disease of idolatrous superstition, were now liberated by the power of Christ, through the teachings and miracles of His messengers (Eusebius, [early fourth century] *Ecclesiastical History,* Book I, ch. 3).

❏ A FALLING AWAY FROM CHRIST'S CHURCH

❏ Apostasy predicted

Behold, the days come, saith the Lord God, that I will send a famine in the land, not a famine of bread, nor a thirst for water, but of hearing the words of the Lord:

And they shall wander from sea to sea, and from the north even to the east, they shall run to and fro to seek the word of the Lord, and shall not find it (Amos 8:11–12).

And Jesus answered and said unto them, Take heed that no man deceive you.

For many shall come in my name, saying, I am Christ; and shall deceive many (Matthew 24:4–5).

For I know this, that after my departing shall grievous wolves enter in among you, not sparing the flock.

Also of your own selves shall men arise, speaking perverse things, to draw away disciples after them (Acts 20:29–30).

Let no man deceive you by any means: for that day shall not come, (the second coming of Christ) except there come a falling away first, and that man of sin be revealed, the son of perdition (2 Thessalonians 2:3).

But there were false prophets also among the people, even as there shall be false teachers among you, who privily shall bring in damnable heresies, even denying the Lord that bought them, and bring upon themselves swift destruction.

And many shall follow their pernicious ways; by reason of whom the way of truth shall be evil spoken of (2 Peter 2:1–2).

I charge thee therefore, before God, and the Lord Jesus Christ, who shall judge the quick and the dead at his appearing and his kingdom;

Preach the word; be instant in season, out of season; reprove, rebuke, exhort with all longsuffering and doctrine.

For the time will come when they will not endure sound doctrine; but after their own lusts shall they heap to themselves teachers, having itching ears;

And they shall turn away their ears from the truth, and shall be turned unto fables (2 Timothy 4:1–4).

The Apostasy documented

Baptism one of the first ordinances changed

History furnishes ample proof that in the first century after the death of Christ, baptism was administered solely by immersion. Tertullian thus refers to the immersion ceremony common in his day: "There is no difference whether one is washed in a sea or in a pool, in a river or in a fountain, in a lake or in a channel; nor is there any difference between those whom John dipped in Jordan, and those whom Peter dipped in the Tiber. . . . We are immersed in the water" (James E. Talmage, *The Great Apostasy,* p. 125).

The mode of baptism underwent a radical change during the first half of the third century. Cyprian, the bishop of Carthage,

6

advocated sprinkling instead of immersion in cases of physical weakness. The practice later became general (Ibid. p. 118).

...We cannot prove that the apostles ordained infant baptism; from those places where the baptism of a whole family is mentioned (Acts 16:33; 1 Cor. 1:16), we can draw no such conclusions, because the inquiry is still to be made whether there were any children in those families of such an age that they were not capable of any intelligent reception of Christianity; for this is the only point on which the case turns (Talmage, p. 126).

"Let them therefore come when they are grown up—when they can understand—when they are taught whither they are to come. Let them become Christians when they can know Christ." (Tertullian, one of the Latin "Christians Fathers." He lived from 150 to 220 A.D.) Tertullian's almost violent opposition to the practice of pedobaptism is cited by Neander as "a proof that it was then not usually considered an apostolic ordinance; for in that case he would hardly have ventured to speak so strongly against it" (Talmage, op. cit., p. 127).

Bishops from large cities rose in rank

"Throughout the first and the greater part of the second century, the Christian churches were independent of each other; nor were they joined together by association other than charity. Late in the second, and throughout the third century distinctions and recognition of rank arose among the bishops, those of large and wealthy cities assuming authority and dignity above that accorded by them to the bishops of the country provinces. The bishops of the largest cities took the title of Metropolitans" (Mosheim, *Ecclesiastical History*, Cent. II, Part II, ch. 2:2–3).

Many unnecessary ceremonies added

"There is no institution so pure and excellent which the corruption and folly of man will not in time alter for the worse, and load with additions foreign to its nature and original design. Such in a particular manner was the fate of Christianity. In this century (the second) many unnecessary rites and ceremonies were added to the Christian worship, the introduction of which was extremely offensive to wise and good men. These changes, while they destroyed the beautiful simplicity of the gospel, were naturally pleasing to the gross multitude, who are more delighted with the pomp and splendor of external institutions than with the native charms of rational and solid piety, and who generally give little attention to any objects but those which strike their outward senses" (Ibid., ch. 4).

Bishops assumed princely authority

"The bishops [during the closing years of the third century] assumed in many places a princely authority, particularly those who had the greatest number of churches under their inspection. . . . They appropriated to their evangelical function the splendid ensigns of temporal majesty. A throne, surrounded with ministers, exalted above his equals the servant of the meek and humble Jesus; and sumptuous garments dazzled the eyes and the minds of the multitude into an ignorant veneration of their arrogated authority (Talmage, *The Great Apostasy,* pp. 94–95).

Bishop of Rome claimed supremacy

Finally the bishop of Rome claimed supremacy. When Constantine made Constantinople the capital of the empire, that bishop claimed equality. For five hundred years the dissension increased, until in 855 A. D. Constantinople disavowed all further allegiance to the bishop of Rome. Today this disruption is marked by the distinction between Roman Catholics and Greek Catholics (Talmage, op. cit., p. 133).

Roman pontiffs claimed the title of Pope

In the eleventh century the Roman pontiffs claimed the right to direct princes, kings, and the affairs of several nations. At this early period of their greatest temporal power the pontiffs took the title of Pope. The power of the popes reached its height in the thirteenth century (Ibid.).

Scriptures only for teachers

The Council of Trent (sixteenth century) prohibited the scriptures from being spoken or explained in different languages. The church of Rome affirmed that the holy scriptures were not composed for the use of the multitude, but only for that of their spiritual teachers. These divine records were ordered to be taken from the people (Talmage, p. 139).

Fictitious stories considered an act of virtue

As early as the fourth century, certain doctrines which disregarded the truth gained popularity in the church. It was taught "that it was an act of virtue to deceive and lie, when by that means the interests of the church might be promoted" (Ibid., Cent. IV, Part II, ch. 3:16).

Many of the fables and fictitious stories relating to the lives of Christ and the apostles, as also the spurious accounts of supernatural visitations and wonderful miracles, in which the literature of the early centuries abound, are traceable to this infamous doctrine that lies are acceptable unto God if perpetrated in a cause that man calls good (Talmage, op. cit., p. 107).

Ashes of martyrs sold as medicinal remedies

In the fourth century the ashes of martyrs as well as dust and earth brought from places said to have been made holy by some uncommon occurrences were sold as remedies against disease and as means of protection against evil spirits (Ibid., p. 114).

People began to worship images

"In the fourth century the adoration of images, pictures, and effigies, had been given a place in the so-called Christian worship. An effort to check the abuses arising from this idolatrous practice in the eighth century, actually led to civil war" (Talmage, p. 115).

Semblance to original church lost

By increasing changes and unauthorized alterations in organization and government, the earthly establishment known as "the Church," with popes, cardinals, abbots, friars, monks, exorcists, acolytes, etc., lost all semblance to the Church as established by Christ and maintained by His apostles (Talmage, op. cit., p. 141).

Apostasy in the western hemisphere

And now, in this two hundred and first year there began to be among them those who were lifted up in pride, such as the wearing of costly apparel, and all manner of fine pearls, and of the fine things of the world.

And from that time forth they did have their goods and their substance no more common among them.

And they began to be divided into classes; and they began to build up churches unto themselves to get gain, and began to deny the true church of Christ.

And it came to pass that when two hundred and ten years had passed away there were many churches in the land; yea, there were many churches which professed to know the Christ, and yet they did deny the more parts of his gospel, insomuch that they did receive all manner of wickedness, and did administer that which was sacred unto him to whom it had been forbidden because of unworthiness.

And this church did multiply exceedingly because of iniquity, and because of the power of Satan who did get hold upon their hearts.

And again, there was another church which denied the Christ; and they did persecute the true church of Christ, because of their humility and their belief in Christ; and they did despise them because of the many miracles which were wrought among them (4 Nephi 1:24–29).

−3−

❏ THE RESTORATION OF THE GOSPEL
OF JESUS CHRIST

❏ Restoration of the Gospel prophesied

And I saw another angel fly in the midst of heaven, having the everlasting gospel to preach unto them that dwell on the earth, and to every nation, and kindred, and tongue, and people, saying with a loud voice, Fear God, and give glory to him; for the hour of his judgment is come: and worship him that made heaven, and earth, and the sea, and the fountains of waters (Revelation 14:6, 7).

And in the days of these kings shall the God of heaven set up a kingdom, which shall never be destroyed: and the kingdom shall not be left to other people, but it shall break in pieces and consume all these kingdoms, and it shall stand for ever (Daniel 2:44).

Then shall they deliver you up to be afflicted, and shall kill you; and ye shall be hated of all nations for my name's sake.
And then shall many be offended, and shall betray one another, and shall hate one another.
And many false prophets shall rise, and shall deceive many.
And because iniquity shall abound, the love of many shall wax cold.

But he that shall endure unto the end, the same shall be saved.

And this gospel of the kingdom shall be preached in all the world for a witness unto all nations; and then shall the end come (Matthew 24:9–14).

Joseph Smith's History

. . . Some time in the second year after our removal to Manchester, there was in the place where we lived an unusual excitement on the subject of religion. It commenced with the Methodists, but soon became general among all the sects in that region of country. Indeed, the whole district of country seemed affected by it, and great multitudes united themselves to the different religious parties, which created no small stir and division amongst the people, some crying, "Lo, here!" and others, "Lo, there!" Some were contending for the Methodist faith, some for the Presbyterian, and some for the Baptist. . . .

I was at this time in my fifteenth year. My father's family was proselyted to the Presbyterian faith, and four of them joined that church, namely, my mother, Lucy; my brothers Hyrum and Samuel Harrison; and my sister Sophronia.

During this time of great excitement my mind was called up to serious reflection and great uneasiness; but though my feelings were deep and often poignant, still I kept myself aloof from all these parties, though I attended their several meetings as often as occasion would permit. . . . It was impossible for a person young as I was, and so unacquainted with men and things, to come to any certain conclusion who was right and who was wrong. . . .

While I was laboring under the extreme difficulties caused by the contests of these parties of religionists, I was one day reading the Epistle of James, first chapter and fifth verse, which reads: If any of you lack wisdom, let him ask of God, that giveth to all men liberally, and upbraideth not; and it shall be given him.

Never did any passage of scripture come with more power to the heart of man than this did at this time to mine. It seemed to enter with great force into every feeling of my heart. I reflected on it again and again, knowing that if any person needed wisdom from God, I did; for how to act I did not know, and unless I could get more wisdom than I then had, I would never know; for the teachers of religion of the different sects understood the same passages of scripture so differently as to destroy all confidence in settling the question by an appeal to the Bible.

At length I came to the conclusion that I must either remain in darkness and confusion, or else I must do as James directs, that is ask of God. I at length came to the determination to "ask of God," concluding that if he gave wisdom to them that lacked wisdom, and would give liberally, and not upbraid, I might venture.

So, in accordance with this, my determination to ask of God, I retired to the woods to make the attempt. It was on the morning of a beautiful, clear day, early in the spring of eighteen hundred and twenty. It was the first time in my life that I had made such an attempt, for amidst all my anxieties I had never as yet made the attempt to pray vocally.

After I had retired to the place where I had previously designed to go, having looked around me, and finding myself alone, I kneeled down and began to offer up the desires of my heart to God. I had scarcely done so, when immediately I was seized upon by some power which entirely overcame me, and had such an astonishing influence over me as to bind my tongue so that I could not speak. Thick darkness gathered around me, and it seemed to me for a time as if I were doomed to sudden destruction.

But, exerting all my powers to call upon God to deliver me out of the power of this enemy which had seized upon me, and at the very moment when I was ready to sink into despair and abandon myself to destruction—not to an imaginary ruin, but to the power of some actual being from the unseen world, who had such marvelous power as I had never before felt in any being—just at this moment of great alarm, I saw a pillar of light exactly over my head, above the brightness of the sun, which descended gradually until it fell upon me.

It no sooner appeared than I found myself delivered from the enemy which held me bound. When the light rested upon me I saw two Personages, whose brightness and glory defy all description, standing above me in the air. One of them spake unto me, calling me by name and said, pointing to the other— This is My Beloved Son. Hear Him!

My object in going to inquire of the Lord was to know which of all the sects was right, that I might know which to join. No sooner, therefore, did I get possession of myself, so as to be able to speak, than I asked the Personages who stood above me in the light, which of all the sects was right (for at this time it had never entered into my heart that all were wrong)—and which I should join.

I was answered that I must join none of them, for they were all wrong; and the Personage who addressed me said that all their creeds were an abomination in his sight; that those professors were all corrupt; that: "they draw near to me with their lips, but their hearts are far from me, they teach for doctrines the commandments of men, having a form of godliness, but they deny the power thereof."

He again forbade me to join with any of them; and many other things did he say unto me, which I cannot write at this time. When I came to myself again, I found myself lying on my back, looking up into heaven. When the light had departed, I had no strength; but soon recovering in some degree, I went home (Joseph Smith—History 1:5–20).

In due time The Church of Jesus Christ of Latter-day Saints was established, the Holy Priesthood having been restored through the ordination of Joseph Smith by those who had held the keys of that authority in former dispensations. The organization of the Church as a body corporate was effected on the sixth day of April, A.D. 1830, at Fayette in the State of New York, and the names of but six persons are of record as those of active participants (James E. Talmage, *Articles of Faith*, p. 15).

Joseph Smith . . . is the prophet and revelator through whom was restored to earth the Gospel of Jesus Christ, in these the last days, the dispensation of the fulness of times, declared and predicted by prophets in earlier dispensations. The question of this man's divine commission is a challenging one to the world today. If his claims to a divine appointment be false, forming as they do the foundation of the Church in this the last dispensation, the superstructure cannot be stable; if, however, his avowed ordination under the hands of heavenly personages be a fact, one need search no farther for the cause of the phenomenal vitality and continuous development of the restored Church (Ibid., p. 7–8).

And he spake to them a parable; Behold the fig tree, and all the trees;
When they now shoot forth, ye see and know of your own selves that summer is now nigh at hand.
So likewise ye, when ye see these things come to pass, know ye that the kingdom of God is nigh at hand (Luke 21:29–31; see also Matthew 24:32–33; Mark 13:28–29).

❏ When the Light shall break forth

And when the light shall begin to break forth, it shall be with them like unto a parable which I will show you—

Ye look and behold the fig-trees, and ye see them with your eyes, and ye say when they begin to shoot forth, and their leaves are yet tender, that summer is now nigh at hand;

Even so it shall be in that day when they shall see all these things, then shall they know that the hour is nigh.

And it shall come to pass that he that feareth me shall be looking forth for the great day of the Lord to come, even for the signs of the coming of the son of Man (D&C 45:36–39).

This parable pertains to the latter-days. The restoration of the gospel, with the light that thereby breaks forth in darkness, is the beginning of the shooting forth of the leaves of the fig tree (Bruce R. McConkie, *Doctrinal New Testament Commentary,* p. 664).

The keys of the kingdom of God are committed unto man on the earth, and from thence shall the gospel roll forth unto the ends of the earth, as the stone which is cut out of the mountain without hands shall roll forth, until it has filled the whole earth (D&C 65:2).

−4−

❏ MISSIONARY WORK

He saith unto him the third time, Simon, son of Jonas, lovest thou me? Peter was grieved because he said unto him the third time, Lovest thou me? And he said unto him, Lord, thou knowest all things; thou knowest that I love thee. Jesus saith unto him, Feed my sheep (John 21:17).

After these things the Lord appointed other seventy also, and sent them two and two before his face into every city and place, whither he himself would come (Luke 10:1)

And when the times of the Gentiles is come in, a light shall break forth among them that sit in darkness, and it shall be the fulness of my gospel (D&C 45:28).

❏ To teach the Gospel

And we did magnify our office unto the Lord, taking upon us the responsibility, answering the sins of the people upon our own heads if we did not teach them the word of God with all diligence; wherefore, by laboring with our might their blood might not come upon our garments; otherwise their blood would come upon our garments, and we would not be found spotless at the last day (Jacob 1:19).

Wherefore, I the Lord, knowing the calamity which should come upon the inhabitants of the earth, called upon my servant Joseph Smith, Jun., and spake unto him from heaven, and gave him commandments;

And also gave commandments to others, that they should proclaim these things unto the world; and all this that it might be fulfilled, which was written by the prophets (D&C 1:17–18).

That the fulness of my gospel might be proclaimed by the weak and the simple unto the ends of the world, and before kings and rulers (D&C 1:23).

❑ A voice of warning

And the voice of warning shall be unto all people, by the mouths of my disciples, whom I have chosen in these last days (D&C 1:4).

Behold, I sent you out to testify and warn the people, and it becometh every man who hath been warned to warn his neighbor (D&C 88:81).

. . . The Lord will, after a while, designate by revelation, and say unto his servants, "It is enough. You have been faithful in laboring in my vineyard, for the last time." . . . It is the eleventh hour, the last warning that will be given to the nations of the earth, first to the Gentiles, and then to the House of Israel (Orson Pratt, JD, Vol. 20:146).

❑ To gather Israel

. . . You shall go to the scattered remnants of the house of Israel. I will gather them in from the four quarters of the earth, and bring them again into their own lands. They shall build Jerusalem on its own heap; they shall rear a Temple on the appointed place in Palestine, and they shall be grafted in again (Orson Pratt, JD, Vol. 18:177).

And ye are called to bring to pass the gathering of mine elect; for mine elect hear my voice and harden not their hearts (D&C 29:7).

❏ The Gospel will spread

Behold, I will send for many fishers, saith the Lord, and they shall fish them; and after will I send for many hunters, and they shall hunt them from every mountain,and from every hill, and out of the holes of the rocks (Jeremiah 16:16).

And I will set my glory among the heathen, and all the heathen shall see my judgment that I have executed, and my hand that I have laid upon them (Ezekiel 39:21–29).

As Joseph's seed brings others into the Church, these new members are then commissioned likewise to go and spread the gospel. . . . "I will take you one of a city, and two of a family, and I will bring you to Zion" (Jer. 3:14). Thus, it is only through the work of thousands of missionaries and millions of Church members that those among the nations who want to return actually "return" (Paul K. Browning, *Ensign,* July 1998, p. 54).

–5–

❏ WARS

And when ye shall hear of wars and rumors of wars, be ye not troubled: for such things must needs be; but the end shall not be yet.

For nation shall rise against nation, and kingdom against kingdom: and there shall be earthquakes in divers places, . . . these are the beginnings of sorrows (Mark 13:7–8).

❏ Beginning at South Carolina

Verily, thus saith the Lord concerning the wars that will shortly come to pass, beginning at the rebellion of South Carolina, which will eventually terminate in the death and misery of many souls;

And the time will come that war will be poured out upon all nations, beginning at this place.

For behold, the Southern States shall be divided against the Northern States, and the Southern States will call on other nations, even the nation of Great Britain, as it is called, and they shall also call upon other nations, in order to defend themselves against other nations; and then war shall be poured out upon all nations. . . .

And thus, with the sword and by bloodshed the inhabitants of the earth shall mourn; and with famine, and plague, and earthquake, and the thunder of heaven, and the fierce and vivid lighting also, shall the inhabitants of the earth be made to feel the wrath, and indignation, and chastening hand of an Almighty God, until the consumption decreed hath made a full end of all nations (D&C 87:1–3, 6).

❑ Japan subdued

I want to say to you that one of the most significant things that I have seen in the Far East is the fulfillment of what Elder Parley P. Pratt testified would be one of the significant developments necessary to the consummation of God's purposes, "The subjugation of Japan and the triumph of constitutional liberty among certain nations where mind and thought and religion are still prescribed by law" (Harold B. Lee, CR, October 1954, p. 126).

❑ Missionaries will preach in Russia

The field that has gone to wild oats needs to be plowed up and harrowed and prepared for a new seed. So in Russia. It may seem appalling to us, but it is God breaking up and destroying an older order of things, and the process will be the accomplishment of God's purposes within a very short period of time, . . . there are thousands of the blood of Israel in that land, and God is preparing the way for them (Melvin J. Ballard, CR, April 1930, p. 157)

A new religious freedom must come. God will overrule it [Communism], for that people must hear the truth and truth in simplicity. Truly there is much for the Church to do in the coming century (David O. McKay, CN, May 28, 1960).

❏ Slaves to rise up against masters

And it shall come to pass, after many days, slaves shall rise up against their masters, who shall be marshaled and disciplined for war (D&C 87:4).

In many cases I am quite sure we all think this has to do particularly with the slaves in the Southern States, but I believe, brethren and sisters, that it was intended that this referred to slaves all over the world, and I think of those, particularly in the land of Russia and other countries wherein they have been taken over by that great nation and where the people are actually the slaves of those individuals who guide and direct the affairs of Russia and China, and where the rights and the privilege to worship God and to come to a knowledge that Jesus Christ is His Son is denied them (Joseph L. Wirthlin, CR, October 1958, p. 32).

❏ Nation against nation

. . . Famine will spread over the nations, and nation will rise up against nations, kingdom against kingdom, and state against states, in our own country and in foreign lands; and they will destroy each other, caring not for the blood and lives of their neighbors, or their families, or for their own lives. They will be like the Jaredites who preceded the Nephites upon this continent, and will destroy each other to the last man, through the anger that the devil will place in their hearts, because they rejected the words of life and are given over to Satan to do whatever he listeth to do with them. You may think that the little you hear of now is grievous; yet the faithful of God's people will see days that will cause them to close their eyes because of the sorrow that will come upon the wicked nations. The hearts of the faithful will be filled with pain and anguish for them (Brigham Young, JD, Vol. 8:123).

❏ Germany to be a prime protagonist

You have scarcely yet read the preface of your national troubles. Many nations will be drawn into the American maelstrom that now whirls through the land; and after many days, when the demon of war shall have exhausted his strength and madness upon American soil, by the destruction of all that can court or provoke opposition, excite cupidity, inspire revenge, or feed ambition, he will remove his headquarters to the banks of the Rhine (Orson Hyde, MS, Vol. 24, May 3, 1862, p. 274).

❏ Thrones will fall

Now, when the times of the Gentiles are fulfilled there will be an uprooting of their governments and institutions, and of their civil, political, and religious polity. There will be a shaking of nations, a downfall of empires, an upturning of thrones and dominions, as Daniel has foretold, and the kingdom and power, and rule on the earth will return to another people, and exist under another polity, as Daniel has further foretold (Parley P. Pratt, JD, Vol. 3:135).

. . . Oh! ye Gentile nations, wake up and prepare yourselves for that which is to come, for as God lives his judgments are at your door. They are at the door of our nation, and the thrones and kingdoms of the whole world will fall, and all the efforts of men combined cannot save them (Wilford Woodruff, JD, Vol. 15:281).

It is not only a Gospel to be preached to all the nations of the earth, but in connection with it you will have to make proclamation connected with it, to all people, to fear God and give glory to him, for the hour of his judgment is come. And as these judgments come, kingdoms and thrones will be cast down and overturned. Empire will war with empire, kingdom with kingdom, and city with city, and there will be one general revolution throughout the earth, the Jews fleeing to their own country, desolation coming upon the wicked, with the swiftness of whirlwinds and fury poured out (Orson Pratt, JD, Vol. 14:65–66).

❏ The bear to lay its paw on the lion

When the great bear [Russia] lays her paw on the lion [England] the winding up scene is not far distant (Joseph Smith, JI, March 15, 1890, p. 162).

Elder Jesse W. Fox, Sen., received the narration from Father Taylor, the father of the late Presidents john Taylor. The old gentleman said that one time the Prophet Joseph was in his house conversing about the battle of Waterloo, in which father Taylor had taken part. Suddenly the Prophet Joseph turned and said, "Father Taylor, you will live to see, though I will not, greater battles than that of Waterloo. The United States will go to war with Mexico, and thus gain an increase of territory. The slave question will cause a division between the North and the South, and in these wars greater battles than Waterloo will occur. "But," he continued, with emphasis, "when the great bear (Russia) lays her paw on the lion (England) the winding up scene is not far distant." (Wilford Woodruff, JI, March 15, 1890, p. 162).

These words were uttered before there was any prospect of war with Mexico, and such a thing as division in the United States was never contemplated. Yes, these fierce struggles came, and though Joseph himself was slain before they occurred, Father Taylor lived to witness some of the world's most remarkable battles.

The struggle between the Bear and the Lion has not yet happened, but as surely as Joseph the Prophet ever predicted such an event so surely will it not fail of its fulfillment (Ibid.).

❏ Missionaries to be called home

When that day shall come (when the missionaries will be called home) there shall be wars, not such wars as have come in centuries and years that are past and gone, but a desolating war. When I say desolating I mean that it will lay these European nations in waste. Cities will be left vacated, without inhabitants. The people will be destroyed by the sword of their own hands. Not only this but many other cities will be burned; for anger, without the Spirit of God upon them, when they have not that spirit of humanity that now characterizes many of the wars amongst the nations, when they are left to themselves, there will be no quarter given, no prisoners taken, but a war of destruction, of desolation, of the burning of the cities and villages, until the land is laid desolate (Orson Pratt, JD, Vol. 20:150–51).

When the testimony of the Elders ceases to be given, and the Lord says to them, "Come home; I will now preach my own sermons to the nations of the earth," all you now know can scarcely be called a preface to the sermon that will be preached with fire and sword, tempests, earthquakes, hail, rain, thunders and lightnings, and fearful destruction. What matters the destruction of a few railway cars? You will hear of magnificent cities, now idolized by the people, sinking in the earth, entombing the inhabitants. The sea will heave itself beyond its bounds, engulphing [sic] mighty cities. Famine will spread over the nations, and nation will rise up against nation, kingdom against kingdom, and states against states, in our own country and in foreign lands; and they will destroy each other, caring not for the blood and lives of their neighbors, of their families, or for their own lives (Brigham Young, JD, Vol. 8:123).

❑ Wars increasing

Out of this study [President Smith referred to a study of wars done by two sociologists] these scientists declare that they have discovered that war has tended to increase over all Europe in the late centuries. They say they have learned that in these countries, war grew from 2,678 in the twelfth century to 13,735.98 in the first twenty-five years of the twentieth century. Their tables show the growth by centuries. Up to the seventeenth century the wars were comparatively insignificant. Beginning with that century war increased during the eighteenth, with a lull in the nineteenth, yet in that century they were more than 100 times greater than in medieval times.

These men conclude that "all commendable hopes that war will disappear in the near future are based on nothing more substantial than hope of a belief in miracles."

And then I made this prediction:

"If prophecy is to be fulfilled, there awaits the world a conflict more dreadful than any the world has yet seen" (*Progress of Man,* pp. 402–4) (Joseph Fielding Smith, *Signs of the Times,* pp. 116, 120–21).

❏ JUDGMENTS WILL BE POURED OUT

❏ An increase in disasters

. . . The world will increase in confusion, doubt and horrible strife. . . . The very elements around will seem to be affected by the national and social convulsions that will agitate the world, and storms, earthquakes, and appalling disasters by sea and land will cause terror and dismay among the people: New diseases will silently eat their ghastly way through the ranks of the wicked (Charles W. Penrose, MS, September 10, 1859).

But we believe that these severe, natural calamities are visited upon men by the Lord for the good of His children, to quicken their devotion to others, and to bring out their better natures, that they may love and serve him. We believe, further, that they are the heralds and tokens of his final judgment, and the schoolmasters to teach the people to prepare themselves, by righteous living, for the coming of the savior to reign upon the earth, when every knee shall bow and every tongue confess that Jesus is the Christ (Joseph F. Smith, IE, June 1906, p. 654).

But the next one-thousand year period will be the earth's sabbath. This will be the period when the earth will rest and enjoy its sanctified state. For this period the earth will be renewed and regain its former status as a terrestrial sphere, with all of its paradisiacal beauty, glory, and righteousness fully restored. But first the earth must be cleansed. During its long history of sin and trouble our earth has become soiled and dirty. And it must have its "Saturday night bath," and be dressed in fresh clean clothing in which it can appropriately live its best 1,000 years (Sterling W. Sill, IE, June 1967, p. 35).

❏ Earthquakes

And the angel took the censer, and filled it with fire of the altar, and cast it into the earth: and there were voices, and thunderings, and lightnings, and an earthquake (Revelation 8:5).

And the seventh angel poured out his vial into the air; and there came a great voice out of the temple of heaven, from the throne, saying, It is done.

And there were voices, and thunders, and lightnings; and there was a great earthquake, such as was not since men were upon the earth, so mighty an earthquake, and so great.

And the great city was divided into three parts, and the cities of the nations fell: and great Babylon came in remembrance before God, to give unto her the cup of the wine of the fierceness of his wrath.

And every island fled away, and the mountains were not found (Revelation 16:17–20).

And there shall be earthquakes also in divers places, and many desolations; yet men will harden their hearts against me, and they will take up the sword, one against another, and they will kill one another (D&C 45:33).

And when that day shall come they (all nations) shall be visited of the Lord of Hosts, with thunder and with earthquake, and with a great noise, and with storm and with tempest, and with the flame of devouring fire (2 Nephi 27:2).

Yea, it [the Book of Mormon] shall come in a day when there shall be heard of fires, and tempests, and vapors of smoke in foreign lands;
And there shall also be heard of wars, rumors of wars, and earthquakes in divers places (Mormon 8:29–30).

O, ye nations of the earth, how often would I have gathered you together as a hen gathereth her chickens under her wings, but ye would not!
How oft have I called upon you by the mouth of my servants, and by the ministering of angels, and by mine own voice, and by the voice of thunderings, and by the voice of lightnings, and by the voice of tempests, and by the voice of earthquakes, and great hailstorms, and by the voice of famines and pestilences of every kind (D&C 43:24–25).

For after your testimony cometh the testimony of earthquakes, that shall cause groanings in the midst of her, and men shall fall upon the ground and shall not be able to stand (D&C 88:89).

❏ Plagues

And I saw another sign in heaven, great and marvellous, seven angels having the seven last plagues; for in them is filled up the wrath of god (Revelation 15:1).

And there shall be men standing in that generation, that shall not pass until they shall see an overflowing scourge; for a desolating sickness shall cover the land.

But my disciples shall stand in holy places, and shall not be moved; but among the wicked, men shall lift up their voices and curse God and die (D&C 45:31–32).

For a desolating scourge shall go forth among the inhabitants of the earth, and shall continue to be poured out from time to time, if they repent not, until the earth is empty, and the inhabitants thereof are consumed away and utterly destroyed by the brightness of my coming (D&C 5:19).

And plagues shall go forth, and they shall not be taken from the earth until I have completed my work, which shall be cut short in righteousness (D&C 84:97).

I was immediately in Salt Lake City wandering about the streets in all parts of the City and On the door of every house I found a badge of mourning, and I could not find a house but what was in mourning. . . .

It seemed strange to me that I saw no person [on] the street in my wandering about through the City. They seemed to be in their houses with their sick and Dead. I saw no funeral procession, or anything of that kind, but the city looked very still and quiet as though the people were praying and had Controll of the disease what ever it was.

I then looked in all directions over the Territory, East west North and South, and I found the same mourning in every place throughout the Land (*A Remarkable Vision* [see appendix])

❏ **Famines**

. . . God hath set his hand and seal to change the times and seasons, and to blind their minds, that they may not understand his marvelous workings (D&C 121:12).

Behold, at my rebuke I dry up the sea. I make the rivers a wilderness; their fish stink, and die for thirst (D&C 133:68–70).

. . . The Lord is not going to disappoint either Babylon or Aion, with regard to famine, pestilence, earthquake or storms, he is not going to disappoint anybody with regard to any of these things, they are at the doors. . . . Lay up your wheat and other provisions against a day of need, for the day will come when they will be wanted, and no mistake about it. We shall want bread, and the Gentiles will want bread, and if we are wise we shall have something to feed them and ourselves when famine comes (Wilford Woodruff, JD, Vol. 18:121).

I have asked of the Lord concerning His coming; and while asking the Lord, He gave a sign and said, "In the days of Noah I set a bow in the heavens as a sign and token that in any year that the bow should be seen the Lord would not come; but there should be seed time and harvest during that year; but whenever you see the bow withdrawn, it shall be a token that there shall be famine, pestilence, and great distress among the nations, and that the coming of the Messiah is not far distant (Joseph Smith, HC, Vol. 6:254).

❏ No safety on the waters

Wherefore the days will come that no flesh shall be safe upon the waters.

And it shall be said in the days to come that none is able to go up to the land of Zion upon the water, but he that is upright in heart (D&C 61:15–16).

❏ Who will suffer the coming judgments?

There is one principle I would like to have the Latter-day Saints perfectly understand—that is, of blessings and cursings. For instance, we read that war, pestilence, plagues, famine, etc., will be visited upon the inhabitants of the earth; but if distress through the judgments of God comes upon this people, it will be because the majority have turned away from the Lord. Let the majority of the people turn away from the Holy Commandments which the Lord has delivered to us, and cease to hold the balance of power in the Church, and we may expect the judgments of God to come upon us; but while six-tenths or three-fourths of this people will keep the commandments of God, the curse and judgments of the Almighty will never come upon them, though we will have trials of various kinds, and the elements to contend with—natural and spiritual elements (Brigham Young, JD, Vol. 10:335).

There is not another people on the earth whose faith and works are directed for the accomplishment of good like the Latter-day Saints. But we do not obey counsel as we should. Yet when we look at them and at others on the face of the earth, we have reason to say we are proud of the Latter-day Saints. But are we all we should be? No. We must learn to listen to the whispering of the Holy Spirit, and the counsels of the servants of God, until we come to the unity of the faith.

There are certain events awaiting the nations of the earth as well as Zion; and when these events overtake us we will be preserved if we take the counsel that is given us and unite our time, labor and means, and produce what we need for our own use; but without this we shall not be prepared to sustain ourselves and we shall suffer loss and inconvenience thereby (Wilford Woodruff, JD, Vol. 17:70).

I explained concerning the coming of the Son of Man; also that it is a false idea that the Saints will escape all the judgments, whilst the wicked suffer; for all flesh is subject to suffer, and "the righteous shall hardly escape;" still many of the Saints will escape, for the just shall live by faith; yet many of the righteous shall fall a prey to disease, to pestilence, etc., by reason of the weakness of the flesh, and yet be saved in the kingdom of God. So that it is an unhallowed principle to say that such and such have transgressed because they have been preyed upon by disease or death, for all flesh is subject to death; and the Savior has said, "Judge not, lest ye be judged" (Joseph Smith, HC, Vol. 4:11).

The Lord's hand is over all, and therein I acknowledge his hand. Not that men are at war, not that nations are trying to destroy nations, not that men are plotting against the liberties of their fellow creatures, not in those respects at all: but God's hand is not shortened. He will control the results that will follow. He will overrule them in a way that you and I, today, do not comprehend, or do not foresee, for ultimate good (Joseph F. Smith, *Teachings of the Presidents of the Church,* p. 394).

7

❏ THE SAINTS AND OTHERS WILL
GATHER TO THE MOUNTAINS

O Zion, that bringest good tidings, get thee up into the high mountain (Isaiah 40:9).

And it shall come to pass in the last days, that the mountain of the Lord's house shall be established in the top of the mountains, and shall be exalted above the hills; and all nations shall flow unto it.

And many people shall go and say, Come ye, and let us go up to the mountain of the Lord, to the house of the God of Jacob; and he will teach us of his ways, and we will walk in his paths: for out of Zion shall go forth the law, and the word of the Lord from Jerusalem (Ibid., 2:2–3).

. . . The Prophet said, "Brethren, I have been very much edified and instructed in your testimonies here tonight, but I want to say to you before the Lord, that you know no more concerning the destinies of this Church and kingdom than a babe upon its mother's lap. You don't comprehend it." I was rather surprised. He said, "It is only a handful of Priesthood you see here tonight, but this Church will fill North and South America—it will fill the world." Among other things he said, "It will fill the Rocky Mountains. There will be tens of thousands of Latter-day Saints who will be gathered in the Rocky Mountains, and there they will open the door for the establishing of the gospel among the Lamanites, who will receive the gospel and their endowments and the blessings of God. This people will go unto the Rocky Mountains; they will there build temples to the Most High. They will raise up a posterity there, and the Latter-day Saints who dwell in these mountains will stand in the flesh until the coming of the Son of Man. The Son of Man will come to them while in the Rocky Mountains" (Wilford Woodruff, CR, April 1898, p. 57).

❑ Gentiles will gather by the thousands

. . . After a while the gentiles will gather by the thousands to this place, and Salt Lake City will be classed among the wicked cities of the world. A spirit of speculation and extravagance will take possession of the Saints, and the results will be financial bondage. Persecution comes next and all true Latter-day Saints will be tested to the limit. Many will apostatize and others will be still not knowing what to do. . . . The Saints will be put to tests that will try the integrity of the best of them. The pressure will become so great that the more righteous among them will cry unto the Lord day and night until deliverance comes (Heber C. Kimball, DN, May 23, 1931).

A flowing stream is one that runs continually; and the Gentiles will, in that day, come to us as a flowing stream, and we shall have to set our gates open continually, they will come as clouds and as doves in large flocks (Orson Pratt, JD, Vol. 3:16).

[Speaking of the recent arrival of some handcart companies] Is this the end of it? No; there will be millions on millions that will come much in the same way, only they will not have hand carts, for they will take their bundles under their arms, and their children on their backs, and under their arms, and flee; and Zion's people will have to send out relief to them, for they will come when the judgments come on the nation (Heber C. Kimball, JD, Vol. 4:106).

❏ Cache Valley will be full

. . . You will have the privilege of going into the towers of a glorious Temple built unto the name of the Most High east of us upon the Logan bench; and while you stand in the towers of the Temple and your eyes survey this glorious valley filled with cities and villages, occupied by tens of thousands of Latter-day Saints, you will then call to mind this visitation of President Young and his company (Wilford Woodruff, DN, Vol. 33, p. 678).

❏ Safety is how we live

I was down in Kelsey, Texas, last November, and I heard a group of anxious people asking, "Is now the day for us to come up to Zion, where we can come to the mountain of the Lord, where we can be protected from our enemies?" I pondered that question. I prayed about it. What should we say to those people who are in their anxiety? I have studied it a bit, I have learned something of what the Spirit has taught, and I know now that the place of safety in this world is not in any given place; it doesn't make so much difference where we live; but the all-important thing is how we live, and I have found that . . . security can come to Israel only when they keep the commandments, when they live so that they can enjoy the companionship, the direction, the comfort, and the guidance of the

Holy "Spirit of the Lord, when they are willing to listen to these men whom God has set here to preside as His mouthpieces, and when we obey the counsels of the Church (Harold B. Lee, CR, April 1943, p. 129).

8

❏ WARS AND DEVASTATION IN
THE UNITED STATES

And now I am prepared to say by the authority of Jesus Christ, that not many years shall pass away before the United States shall present such a scene of blood shed as has not a parallel in the history of our nation; pestilence, hail, famine, and earthquake will sweep the wicked of this generation from off the face of the land, to open and prepare the way for the return of the lost tribes of Israel from the north country (Joseph Smith, HC, 1:315)

❏ City against city

It will be a war of neighborhood against neighborhood, city against city, town against town, county against county, state against state, and they will go forth, destroying and being destroyed and manufacturing will, in a great measure, cease, for a time among the American nation. . . . There will be too much bloodshed, too much mobocracy, too much going forth in bands and destroying and pillaging the land to suffer people to pursue any local vocation with any degree of safety (Orson Pratt, JD, Vol. 20:151).

❏ The government to be overthrown

. . . I prophesy in the name of the Lord God of Israel, unless the United States redress the wrongs committed upon the Saints in the state of Missouri and punish the crimes committed by her officers that in a few years the government will be utterly overthrown and wasted, and there will not be so much as a potsherd left (Joseph Smith, HC, Vol. 5:394).

I warn future historians to give credence to my history; for my testimony is true, and the truth of its record will be manifest in the world to come. All the words of the Lord will be fulfilled upon the nations, which are written in this book. The American nation will be broken in pieces like a potter's vessel, and will be cast down to hell if it does not repent—and this, because of murders, whoredoms, wickedness and all manner of abominations, for the Lord has spoken it. (Matthias F. Cowley, *Wilford Woodruff*, p. 500).

❏ **The constitution will be in danger**

When the people shall have torn to shreds the Constitution of the United States the Elders of Israel will be found holding it up to the nations of the earth and proclaiming liberty and equal rights to all men, and extending the hand of fellowship to the oppressed of all nations. This is part of the program, and as long as we do what is right and fear God, he will help us and stand by us under all circumstances (John Taylor, JD, Vol. 21:8).

. . . Concerning the United States, the Lord revealed to his prophets that its greatest threat would be a vast, world-wide secret combination which would not only threaten the United States but seek to overthrow the freedom of all lands, nations and countries. In connection with the attack on the United states, the Lord told his prophet there would be an attempt to overthrow the country by destroying the Constitution. Joseph

Smith predicted that the time would come when the Constitution would hang, as it were, by a thread, and at that time this people will step forth and save it from the threatened destruction. It is my conviction that the Elders of Israel, widely spread over the nation, will at that crucial time successfully rally the righteous of our country and provide the necessary balance of strength to save the institutions of constitutional government (Ezra Taft Benson, CR, October 7, 1961)

Will the Constitution be destroyed? No: it will be held inviolate by this people; and, as Joseph Smith said, "The time will come when the destiny of the nation will hang upon a single thread. At that critical juncture, this people will step forth and save it from the threatened destruction." It will be so (Brigham Young, JD, Vol. 7:15).

❏ A remnant of Jacob among the Gentiles

Therefore, repent ye [the Gentiles], and humble yourselves before him, lest he shall come out in justice against you— lest a remnant of the seed of Jacob (the American Indians or Lamanites) shall go forth among you as a lion, and tear you in pieces, and there is none to deliver (Mormon 5:24).

Therefore it shall come to pass that whosoever will not believe in my words, who am Jesus christ, which the father shall cause him to bring forth unto the Gentiles, and shall give unto him power that he shall bring them forth unto the Gentiles, (it shall be done even as Moses said) they shall be cut off from among my people who are of the covenant.
And my people who are a remnant of Jacob shall be among the gentiles, yea, in the midst of them as a lion among the beasts of the forest, as a young lion among the flocks of

sheep, who, if he go through both treadeth down and teareth in pieces, and none can deliver.

Their hand shall be lifted up upon their adversaries, and all their enemies shall be cut off (3 Nephi 21:11–13)

❏ Destruction of great cities

. . . You will say: That was in the days when Presidents Benson and Maughan presided over us; that was before New York was destroyed by an earthquake. It was before Boston was swept into the sea, by the sea heaving itself beyond its bounds; it was before Albany was destroyed by fire; yea, at that time you will remember the scenes of this day. Treasure them up and forget them not. President Young followed and said: "What Brother Woodruff has said is revelation and will be fulfilled" (Wilford Woodruff [a sermon delivered in Logan, Utah, on August 22, 1863], DN, 33:678).

❏ The Rocky Mountains will be a place of safety

We are blessed in these mountains; this is the best place on earth for the Latter-day Saints. . . . You cannot find another situation so well adapted for the Saints as are these mountains. Here is the place in which the Lord designed to hide His people. . . . It has been designed, for many generations, to hide up the Saints in the last days, until the indignation of the Almighty be over.

His wrath will be poured out upon the nations of the earth (Brigham Young, DN, Vol. 11, No. 9, May 1, 1861).

❏ The influx of people will bring the danger of famine

. . . Lay up your wheat and other provision against a day of need, for the day will come when they will be wanted, and no

46

mistake about it. . . . We shall want bread, and the Gentiles will want bread, and if we are wise we shall have something to feed them and ourselves when famine comes (Wilford Woodruff, JD, Vol. 18:121).

❏ The Rocky Mountains will be cut off from the rest of the country

Lay up your stores, and take your silks and fine things, and exchange them for grain and such things as you need, and the time will come when we will be obliged to depend upon our own resources; for the time is not far distant when the curtain will be dropped between us and the United States. When the time comes, brethren and sisters, you will wish you had commenced sooner to make your own clothing. I tell you, God requires us to go into home manufacture; and, prolong it as much as you like, you have got to do it (Heber C. Kimball, JD, Vol. 5:10).

9

❏ THE JEWS WILL GATHER TO THE HOLY LAND

We all know that from the time of the destruction of Jerusalem in the year 70 A.D. until near the close of World War I, Jerusalem was trodden down of the Gentiles, and during all of that time the Jews were scattered and almost without privileges in the Holy Land. The Lord said they should remain scattered among the nations until the times of the Gentiles were fulfilled. Moroni said the times of the Gentiles were about to be fulfilled. Today we are living in the transition period; the day of the Gentiles has come in, and the day of Judah and the remnant of downtrodden Israel is now at hand. The sign for the fulfillment of the prophecy has been given (Joseph Fielding Smith, *Doctrines of Salvation,* Vol. 3:258–59).

. . . The Lord has decreed that the Jews should be gathered from all the Gentile nations where they have been driven, into their own land, in fulfillment of the words of moses their law-giver. And this is the will of your great Elohim, O house of Judah, and when ever you shall be called upon to perform this work, the God of Israel will help you. You have a great future and destiny before you and you cannot avoid fulfilling it; you are the royal chosen seed, and the God of your father's house has kept you distinct as a nation for eighteen hundred years, under all the oppression of the whole Gentile world. You may not wait until you believe on Jesus of Nazareth, but when you meet with Shiloh your king, you will know him; your destiny is marked out, you cannot avoid it (Matthias F. Cowley, *Wilford Woodruff,* pp. 509–10).

❏ The Holy Land dedicated

On October 24, 1841, Orson Hyde, a Jewish disciple of the latter-day Church, journeyed to the city of old Jerusalem, and from the summit of the Mount of Olives poured from his heart a prayer of dedication unto the Lord (Joseph Fielding Smith, *Essentials of Church History,* p. 284).

In 1873, George A. Smith was sent by President Brigham Young to again dedicate the land and pray that the Lord's work might be hastened unto an opening of the way for the return of the exiled Jews (*Complete History of the Church,* vol. 5:474–75).

❏ Palestine set apart for a Jewish homeland

In 1917, as a product of the First World War, for the first time in eighteen centuries, the ancient promised land fell into the hands of a government with a sympathetic understanding of the Jewish problem. The territory of Palestine was inhabited by bitterly antagonistic Arabs, but it was set apart for a Jewish home-land (H.G. Wells, *Outline of History,* pp. 1122–23).

❏ They will build up the wastelands

And they shall build the old wastes, they shall raise up the former desolations, and they shall repair the waste cities, the desolations of many generations (Isaiah 61:4).

And I will bring again the captivity of my people Israel, and they shall build the waste cities, and inhabit them; and they shall plant vineyards, and drink the wine thereof; they shall also make gardens, and eat the fruit of them (Amos 9:14).

In a writing issued recently this statement was made:
"About two million Jews have returned to restore land which has lain desolate for centuries. In little more than ten years fetid swamps have been transformed into fertile valleys. Orchards now blossom on stony hillsides. Farms have sprouted in the desert and towns and cities have been built on the site of ancient settlements." (Know the World: Israel, "Around the World Program" by Peggy Mann.) . . .

In 1948, with a population of 600,000 the Declaration of Independence was issued, and the State of Israel was established. An army of 35,000 Jews was opposed by an army of nearly 80,000 Arabs. In about nine months peace was declared and they set up their government. They planted more than 53 million trees. Martyrs' Forest has six million trees, one for each Jewish life lost in Nazi Europe.

This statement by a writer is very interesting:
"Strangely enough when the State of Israel was reborn in 1948, it was a nation of 600,000, the same number which the Bible reports that Moses led out of bondage in Egypt. It now numbers some two million, the same number which it is said populated the ancient Kingdom of Solomon, when Israel was in all its glory." (See above reference)

That is why we may now say that the Jews have returned to Palestine. On a land one-tenth the size of Utah they have nearly a half million more people than we have in our whole Church [1960] (George Q. Morris, CR, April 1960, p. 101).

❏ The temple at Jerusalem will be rebuilt

There will be a great temple erected within her walls (Revelation 11:1–2).

I wish in this testimony to say that the time is not far distant when the rich men among the Jews will be called upon to use their abundant wealth to gather the dispersed of Judah, and purchase the ancient dwelling places of their fathers in and about Jerusalem, and rebuild the holy city and temple (Ibid., p. 509).

Judah must return, Jerusalem must be rebuilt, and the temple, and water come out from under the temple and the waters of the Dead Sea be healed. It will take some time to rebuild the walls of the city and the temple etc.; and all this must be done before the Son of Man will make His appearance (Joseph Smith, HC, Vol. 5:337).

For a description of the temple, see Ezekiel 40–47.

❏ The battle of Armageddon

. . . When the Rothschilds and the great bankers among the Jewish nation shall return back to their own land to rebuild the city of Jerusalem, carrying their capital with them, it will almost ruin some of the nations, and the latter will go up against Jerusalem to take a spoil (Orson Pratt, JD, Vol. 14:352).

The bankrupt nations, envying the wealth of the sons of Judah, will seek a pretext to make war upon them, and will invade the "holy land" to "take a prey and a spoil." . . .

After the Kingdom of God has spread upon the face of the earth, and every jot and tittle of the prophecies have been fulfilled in relation to the spreading of the Gospel among the nations,—after signs have been shown in the heavens above, and on the earth beneath, blood, fire, and vapor of smoke,— after the sun is turned into darkness, and the moon shall have the appearance of blood, and the stars have apparently been hurled out of their places, and all things have been in commotion, so great will be the darkness resting upon Christendom, and so great the bonds of priestcraft with which they will be bound, that they will not understand, and they will be given up to the hardness of their hearts. Then will be fulfilled that saying, That the day shall come when the Lord shall have power over his Saints, and the Devil shall have power over his own dominion. He will give them up to the power of the Devil, and he will have power over them, and he will carry them about as chaff before a whirlwind. He will gather up millions upon millions of people into the valleys around about Jerusalem in order to destroy the jews after they have gathered. How will the Devil do this? He will perform miracles to do it. The Bible says the kings of the earth and the great ones will be deceived by these false miracles. It says there shall be three unclean spirits that shall go forth working miracles, and they are spirits of devils. Where do they go? To the kings of the earth; and what will they do? Gather them up to battle unto the great day of God Almighty. Where: Into the valley of Armageddon (Orson Pratt JD, Vol. 7:188–89).

. . . The valley of Armageddon is located about sixty miles northwest of Jerusalem. This place is also called the Valley of Decision (NPM).

Thou shalt come up against my people of Israel, as a cloud to cover the land; it shall be in the latter days and I will bring thee against my land . . . (Ezekiel 38:16).

John, the revelator, told the number of their ranks. They

totaled 200,000,000 (Revelation ch. 9).

. . . It is true that after you return and gather your nation home, and rebuild your City and Temple, that the Gentiles may gather together their armies to go against you to battle, to take you a prey and to take you as a spoil, which they will do, for the words of your prophets must be fulfilled; but when this affliction comes, the living God that led Moses through the wilderness, will deliver you, and your Shiloh will come and stand in your midst and fight your battles; and you will know him, and the afflictions of the Jews will be at an end, while the destruction of the Gentiles will be so great that it will take the whole house of Israel who are gathered about Jerusalem, seven months to bury the dead of their enemies, and the weapons of war will last them seven years for fuel, so that they need not go to any forest for wood (Matthias F. Cowley, *Wilford Woodruff*, pp. 509–10).

❏ Two missionaries

Q. What is to be understood by the two witnesses, in the eleventh chapter of Revelations?
A. They are two prophets that are to be raised up to the Jewish nation in the last days, at the time of the restoration, and to prophesy to the Jews after they are gathered and have built the city of Jerusalem in the land of their fathers (D&C 77:15).

John in his 11th chapter of Revelation, gives us many more particulars concerning this same event. He informs us that, after the city and temple are rebuilt by the Jew, the Gentiles will tread it under foot forty and two months, during which time there will be two Prophets continually prophesying and working mighty miracles. And it seems that the Gentile army shall be hindered from utterly destroying and overthrowing the city, while these two Prophets continue. But, after a struggle of three years and a half, they at length succeed in destroying these two Prophets, and then over-running much of the city, they send gifts to each other because of the death of the two Prophets, and in the meantime will not allow their dead bodies to be put in graves, but suffer them to lie in the streets of Jerusalem three days and a half, during which the armies of the Gentiles, consisting of many kindreds, tongues and nations, passing through the city, plundering the Jews, see their dead bodies lying in the street. But after three days and a half, on a sudden, the spirit of life from God enters them, and they will rise and stand upon their feet, and great fear will fall upon them that see them. And then they shall hear a voice from heaven saying, "Come up hither," and they will ascend up to heaven in a cloud, and their enemies beholding them (Parley P. Pratt, *A Voice of Warning*, pp. 41–42).

But the court which is without the temple leave out, and measure it not; for it is given unto the Gentiles: and the holy city shall they tread under foot forty and two months.

And I will give power unto my two witnesses [Isaiah 51:19–20; Zechariah 4:14; and D&C 133:58], and they shall prophesy a thousand two hundred and threescore days, clothed in sackcloth. These are the two olive trees, and the two candlesticks standing before the God of the earth.

And if any man will hurt them, fire proceedeth out of their mouth, and devoureth their enemies: and if any man will hurt them, he must in this manner be killed.

These have power to shut heaven, that it rain not in the days of their prophecy: and have power over waters to turn them to blood, and to smite the earth with all plagues, as often as they will.

And when they shall have finished their testimony, the beast that ascendeth out of the bottomless pit shall make war against them, and shall overcome them, and kill them.

And their dead bodies shall lie in the street of the great city, which spiritually is called Sodom and Egypt, where also our Lord was crucified.

And they of the people and kindreds and tongues and nations shall see their dead bodies three days and an half, and shall not suffer their dead bodies to be put in graves.

And they that dwell upon the earth shall rejoice over them, and make merry, and shall send gifts one to another; because these two prophets tormented them that dwelt on the earth.

And after three days and an half the Spirit of life from God entered into them, and they stood upon their feet; and great fear fell upon them which saw them.

And they heard a great voice from heaven saying unto them, Come up hither. And they ascended up to heaven in a cloud; and their enemies beheld them (Revelations 11:2–12).

❏ Christ will stand on the Mount of Olives

And his feet shall stand in that day upon the mount of Olives, which is before Jerusalem on the east, and the mount of Olives shall cleave in the midst thereof toward the east and toward the west, and there shall be a very great valley: and half of the mountain shall remove toward the north, and half of it toward the south (Zechariah 14:4–5).

Then shall the arm of the Lord fall upon the nations.
And then shall the Lord set his foot upon this mount, and

it shall cleave in twain, and the earth shall tremble, and reel to and fro, and the heavens also shall shake (D&C 45:47–50).

His (Christ's) next appearance (after the temple in the New Jerusalem) will be among the distressed and nearly vanquished sons of Judah. At the crisis of their fate, when the hostile troops of several nations are ravaging the city and all the horrors of war are overwhelming the people of Jerusalem, he will set his feet upon the Mount of Olives, which will cleave and part asunder at his touch. Attended by a host from heaven, he will overthrow and destroy the combined armies of the Gentiles, and appear to the worshipping Jews as the mighty Deliverer and Conquerer so long expected by their race (Charles W. Penrose, MS, Vol. 21:583, Sept. 10, 1859).

All of them (the prophets) speak of it; and when that time comes, the Lord is going to come out of His hiding place. You can see what a terrible condition it is going to be; and the Jews besieged, not only in Jerusalem, but, of course, all through Palestine are in the siege; and when they are about to go under, then the Lord comes. There will be the great earthquake. The earthquake will not be only in Palestine. There will not be merely the separation of the Mount of Olives, to form a valley that the Jews may escape, but the whole earth is going to be shaken. There will be some dreadful things take place, and some great changes are going to take place, and that you will find written in the book of Ezekiel 938:17–23), which I did not read to you (Joseph Fielding Smith, *Signs of the Times,* p. 170).

❏ David, the Prince

Although David was a king, he never did obtain the spirit and power of Elijah and the fullness of the Priesthood; and the

Priesthood that he received, and the throne and kingdom of David is to be taken from him and given to another by the name of David in the last days, raise up out of his lineage (*Teachings of the Prophet Joseph Smith,* p. 339).

. . . He shall build the temple of the Lord; and he shall bear the glory, and shall sit and rule upon His throne; And he shall be a priest upon his throne (Zechariah 6:11–13; Jeremiah 23:5–6; Hosea 3:4–5).

And I will set up one shepherd over them, and he shall feed them, even my servant David; he shall feed them, and he shall be their shepherd.
And I Lord will be their God, and my servant David a prince among them; I the Lord have spoken it (Ezekiel 34:23-24).

Afterward shall the children of Israel return, and seek the Lord their God, and David their king; and shall fear the Lord and his goodness in the latter days (Hosea 3:5).

❏ Christ will come to the temple in Jerusalem

Then he brought me back the way of the gate of the outward sanctuary which looketh toward the east; and it was shut.
Then said the Lord unto me; This gate shall be shut, it shall not be opened, and no man shall enter in by it; because the Lord, the God of Israel, hath entered in by it, therefore it shall be shut.
It is for the prince (David); the prince, he shall sit in it to eat bread before the Lord; he shall enter by the way of the porch of that gate, and shall go out by the way of the same (Ezekiel 44:1–3).

58

And then shall the Jews look upon me and say: What are these wounds in thine hands and in thy feet?

Then shall they know that I am the Lord: for I will say unto them: These wounds are the wounds with which I was wounded in the house of my friends. I am he who was lifted up. I am Jesus that was crucified. I am the Son of God (D&C 45:51–52).

10

❏ ADAM-ONDI-AHMAN

❏ Adam is at the head of all nations

Three years previous to the death of Adam, he called Seth, Enos, Cainan, Mahalaleel, Jared, Enoch, and Methuselah, who were all high priests, with the residue of his posterity who were righteous, into the valley of Adam-ondi-Ahman, and there bestowed upon them his last blessing.

And the Lord appeared unto them, and they rose up and blessed Adam, and called him Michael, the prince, the archangel.

And the Lord administered comfort unto Adam, and said unto him: I have set thee to be at the head; a multitude of nations shall come of thee, and thou art a prince over them forever.

And Adam stood up in the midst of the congregation; and, notwithstanding he was bowed down with age, being full of the Holy Ghost, predicted whatsoever should befall his posterity unto the latest generation.

These things were all written in the book of Enoch, and are to be testified of in due time (D&C 107:53–57).

❏ The Ancient of Days

Spring Hill is named by the Lord Adam-ondi-Ahman, because, said he, it is the place where Adam shall come to visit his people, or the Ancient of Days shall sit, as spoken of by Daniel the prophet (D&C 116:1).

That you may come up unto the crown prepared for you, and be made rulers over many kingdoms, saith the Lord God, the Holy One of Zion, who hath established the foundations of Adam-ondi-Ahman (D&C 78:15).

❏ A council to be called

I beheld till the thrones were cast down, and the Ancient of days did sit, whose garment was white as snow, and the hair of his head like the pure wool: his throne was like the fiery flame, and his wheels as burning fire.

A fiery stream issued and came forth from before him: thousand thousands ministered unto him, and ten thousand times ten thousand stood before him: the judgment was set, and the books were opened (Daniel 7:9–10).

Daniel in his seventh chapter speaks of the Ancient of days; he means the oldest man, our Father Adam, Michael, he will call his children together and hold a council with them to prepare them for the coming of the Son of Man. He (Adam) is the father of the human family, and presides over the spirits of all men, and all that have had the keys must stand before him in this grand council. This may take place before some of us leave this stage of action. The Son of Man stands before him, and there is given him glory and dominion. Adam delivers up his stewardship to Christ, that which was delivered to him as holding the keys of the universe, but retains his standing as head of the human family (Joseph Smith, HC, 3:386–87).

The location of Adam-ondi-Ahman

In the afternoon I went up the river about half a mile to Wight's Ferry, accompanied by President Rigdon, and my clerk,

George W. Robinson, for the purpose of selecting and laying claim to a city plat near said ferry in Daviess County, township 60, ranges 27 and 28, and sections 25, 36, 31, and 10, which the brethren called "Spring Hill," but by the mouth of the Lord it was named Adam-ondi-Ahman, because, said He, it is the place where Adam shall come to visit his people, or the Ancient of Days shall sit, as spoken of by Daniel the Prophet (Joseph Smith, HC, Vol. 3:35).

❑ The keys of all dispensations given to Christ

Not many years hence there shall be another gathering of high priests and righteous souls in this same valley of Adam-ondi-Ahman. At this gathering Adam, the Ancient of Days, will again be present. At this time the vision which Daniel saw will be enacted. The Ancient of Days will sit. There will stand before him those who have held the keys of all dispensations, who shall render up their stewardships to the first Patriarch of the race, who holds the keys of salvation. This shall be a day of judgment and preparation. . . .

This council in the valley of Adam-ondi-Ahman is to be of the greatest importance to this world. At that time there will be a transfer of authority from the usurper and impostor, Lucifer, to the rightful King, Jesus Christ. Judgment will be set and all who have held keys will make their reports and deliver their stewardships, as they shall be required. Adam will direct this judgment, and then he will make his report, as the one holding the keys for this earth, to his Superior Officer, Jesus Christ. Our Lord will then assume the reins of government; directions will be given to the Priesthood there assembled. This grand council of priesthood will be composed, not only of those who are faithful who now dwell on this earth, but also of the prophets and apostles of old, who have had directing authority. Others may also be there, but if so they will be there by appointment, for this is to be an official council called to attend to the most momentous matters concerning the destiny of this earth (Joseph Fielding Smith, *The Way to Perfection,* pp. 289–91).

. . . All the various quorums and councils of the Priesthood in every dispensation that has transpired since the days of Adam until the present time will find their places, according to the callings, gifts, blessings, ordinations and keys of Priesthood which the Lord Almighty has conferred upon them in their several generations. This, then, will be one of the grandest meetings that has ever transpired upon the face of our globe (Orson Pratt, JD, Vol. 17:187–88).

❑ Only those in attendance will know of it

When this gathering is held, the world will not know of it; the members of the Church at large will no know of it, yet it shall be preparatory to the coming in the clouds of glory of our Savior Jesus Christ as the Prophet Joseph Smith has said. The world cannot know it. The Saints cannot know it—except those who officially shall be called into this council—for it shall precede the coming of Jesus Christ as a thief in the night, unbeknown to all the world (Joseph Fielding Smith, *The Way to Perfection,* p. 291).

The valley is being prepared

At this time the valley of Adam-ondi-Ahman has been almost completely prepared for the great council and the coming of the Ancient of Days (Adam). The Church has bought all the property in the valley. Missionary couples with special skills have been called to help plan and prepare the land. Old buildings have been torn down and rusting cars and other trash have been hauled off or buried. The awful thorn trees that filled the valley have all been removed, and sod and lovely trees indigenous to the area have been planted (NPM).

11

❑ A TIME OF PERSECUTION AND SIFTING

❑ A test is coming

Heber C. Kimball gave this warning:

We think we are secure here in the chambers of the ever-lasting hills, where we can close those few doors of the canyons against mobs and persecutors, the wicked and the vile, who have always beset us with violence and robbery, but I want to say to you, my brethren, the time is coming when we will be mixed up in these now peaceful valleys to that extent that it will be difficult to tell the face of a Saint from the face of an enemy to the people of God. Then, brethren, look out for the great sieve, for there will be a great sifting time, and many will fall; for I say unto you there is a test, a TEST, a TEST coming, and who will be able to stand? (Orson F. Whitney, *Life of Heber C. Kimball,* p. 446).

❑ We cannot endure on borrowed light

This Church has before it many close places through which it will have to pass before the work of God is crowned with victory. To meet the difficulties that are coming, it will be necessary for you to have a knowledge of the truth of this work for yourselves. The difficulties will be of such a character that the man or woman who does not possess this personal knowledge or witness will fall. If you have not got the testimony, live right and call upon the Lord and cease not till you obtain it. If you do not you will not stand.

Remember these sayings, for many of you will live to see them fulfilled. The time will come when no man nor woman will be able to endure on borrowed light. Each will have to be guided by the light within himself. If you do not have it, how can you stand? Do you believe it?. . . .

. . . You will have all the persecution you want and more too, and all the opportunity to show your integrity to God and truth that you could desire (Ibid., pp. 449–50, 451).

. . . The time will come when the government will stop the Saints from holding meetings. When this is done the Lord will pour out His judgments (Ibid., p. 442).

❏ Persecution follows financial bondage

Persecution comes next (after financial bondage) and all true Latter-day Saints will be tested to the limit...many will apostatize and others will stand still, not knowing what to do. Darkness will cover the earth and gross darkness the minds of the people...

...the Saints will be put to tests that will try the integrity of the best of them. The pressure will become so great that the more righteous among them will cry unto the Lord day and night until deliverance comes (Heber C. Kimball, DN, May 23, 1931).

Brethren, let us think about that (the cost of sacrificing the principles of the Constitution) because I say unto you with all the soberness I can, that we stand in danger of losing our liberties, and that once lost, only blood will bring them back; and once lost, we of this church will, in order to keep the church going forward, have more sacrifices to make and more persecutions to endure than we have yet known, heavy as our sacrifices and grievous as our persecutions of the past have been (J. Reuben Clark Jr., IE, May 1944, p. 337).

❏ Nations of the earth against the kingdom of God

If we live, we shall see the nations of the earth arrayed against this people; for that time must come in fulfillment of prophecy. Tell about war commencing! Bitter and relentless war was waged against Joseph Smith before he had received the plates of the Book of Mormon; and from that time till now the wicked have only fallen back at times to gain strength and learn how to attack the Kingdom of God (Brigham Young, JD, Vol. 5:339).

❏ Stand in holy places

My disciples shall stand in holy places, and shall not be moved (D&C 45:32).

Wherefore, lift up your hearts and rejoice, and gird up your loins, and take upon you my whole armor, that ye may be able to withstand the evil day, having done all, that ye may be able to stand (D&C 27:15).

We . . . live in the midst of economic, political and spiritual instability. When these signs are observed—unmistakable evidences that His coming is nigh—we need not be troubled, but "stand in holy places, and be not moved, until the day of the Lord come" (D&C 87:8). Holy men and women stand in holy places, and these holy places consist of our temples, our chapels, our homes, and stakes of Zion, which are, as the Lord declares, "for a defense, and for a refuge from the storm, and from wrath when it shall be poured out without mixture upon the whole earth" (D&C 115:6). We must heed the Lord's counsel to the Saints of this dispensation: "Prepare yourselves for the great day of the Lord" (D&C 133:10). This preparation must consist of more than just casual membership in the church. We must be guided by personal revelation and the counsel of the living prophet so we will not be deceived. Our Lord has indicated who, among Church members, will stand when He appears: "At that day, when I shall come in my glory, shall the parable be fulfilled which I spake concerning the ten virgins" (D&C 45:56). There is a real sifting going on in the Church, and it is going to become more pronounced with the passing of time. It will sift the wheat from the tares, because we face some difficult days, the like of which we have never experienced in our lives. And those days are going to require faith and testimony and family unity, the like of which we have never had (*The Teachings of Ezra Taft Benson,* pp. 106–7).

12

❏ THE NEW JERUSALEM

❏ The western boundary of Missouri to be swept clean

The Lord will "purge the land . . . cut off the evil doer, and prepare a way for the return of my [His] people to their inheritance," . . . "if our enemies do not cease their oppression upon this people, as sure as the Lord lives it will not be many days before we will occupy that land [of Zion] and there build up a Temple to the Lord" (Brigham Young, JD, Vol. 9:270).

The judgments of God will be poured out upon the wicked to that extent that our Elders from far and near will be called home, or, in other word, the Gospel will be taken from the Gentiles and later on will be carried to the Jews. The western boundaries of the state of Missouri will be swept so clean of its inhabitants that as President Young tells us, when we return to that place there will not be so much as a yellow dog to wag his tail. Before that day comes, however, the Saints will be put to the test that will try the best of them. The pressure will be so great that the righteous among us will cry unto the Lord day and night until deliverance comes. Then the Prophet Joseph and others will make their appearance and those who have remained faithful will be selected to return to Jackson County, Missouri and take part in the upbuilding of that beautiful city, the New Jerusalem (Heber C. Kimball, DN, May 23, 1931).

❏ A leader like unto Moses

Therefore, I will raise up unto my people a man, who shall lead them like as Moses led the children of Israel (D&C 103:16).

. . . Indeed, before we can go back to inherit this land in all its fulness of perfection, God has promised that he would raise up a man like unto Moses. Who this man will be I do not know; it may be a person with whom we are entirely unacquainted; it may be one of our infant children; it may be some person not yet born; it may be some one of middle age. But suffice it to say, that God will raise up such a man, and he will show forth his power through him, and through the people that he will lead forth to inherit that country, as he did through our fathers in the wilderness (Orson Pratt, JD, Vol. 21:153).

And it shall come to pass that I, the Lord God, will send one mighty and strong, holding the scepter of power in his hand, clothed with light for a covering, whose mouth shall utter words, eternal words; while his bowels shall be a fountain of truth, to set in order the house of God, and to arrange by lot the inheritances of the saints whose names are found, and the names of their fathers, and of their children, enrolled in the book of the law of God (D&C 85:7).

The following has been issued by the Presidency of the Church of Jesus Christ of Latter-day Saints in explanation of verses 7 and 8 of section 85 of the Doctrine and Covenants, and is to be received as authoritative.

One would think in such a matter as this that sufficient native modesty would assert itself to restrain a man from announcing himself as the one upon whom such high honors are to be conferred, and who is to exercise such great powers in establishing the Saints in their inheritances; and that even if one suspected, for any reason, that such a position, and such exceptional powers were to be conferred upon him, he would wait until the Lord would clearly indicate to the Church, as well as to himself, that he had indeed been sent of God to do the work of so noble a ministry, as is described in the passage under question. Those, however, who have so far proclaimed themselves as being the one "mighty and strong," have manifested the utmost ignorance of the things of God and the order of the Church. Indeed their insufferable ignorance and egotism have been at the bottom of all their pretensions, and the cause of all the trouble into which they have fallen. They seem not to have been aware of the fact that the Church of Christ and of the Saints is completely organized, and that when the man who shall be called upon to divide unto the Saints their inheritances comes, he will be designated by the inspiration of the Lord to the proper authorities of the Church, appointed and sustained according to the order provided for the government of the Church. So long as that Church remains in the earth—and we have the assurance from the Lord that it will now remain in the earth forever—the Saints need look for nothing of God's appointing that will be erratic, or irregular, or that smacks of starting over afresh or that would ignore or overthrow the established order of things ("One Mighty and Strong," Official statement by the First Presidency, IE, October 1907, pp. 929–31).

❏ A command to return

. . . Well then, to return to the prophesying, when the time shall come that the Lord shall waste away this nation, he will give commandment to this people to return and possess their own inheritance which they purchased some forty-four years ago in the state of Missouri (Orson Pratt, DEN, Vol. 8, No. 265, Oct. 2, 1875).

When God leads the people back to Jackson County, how will he do it? Let me picture to you how some of us may be gathered and led to Jackson County. I think I see two or three hundred thousand people wending their way across the great plain enduring the nameless hardships of the journey, herding and guarding their cattle by day and by night, and defending themselves and little ones from foes on the right hand and on the left, as when they came here (Joseph F. Smith, JD, Vol. 24:156–57).

. . . We do not expect that when the time shall come, that all Latter-day Saints, who now occupy the mountain valleys, will go in one consolidated body, leaving this land totally without inhabitants. We do no expect any such thing (Orson Pratt JD, Vol. 21:149).

. . . There is one thing certain—something that you and I may depend upon, with as much certainty as we expect to get our daily food, and that is, that the Lord our God will take this people back, and will select from among this people, a sufficient number, to make the army of Israel very great. And when that day comes, he will guide the forces of those who emigrate to their possessions in those two states, that I have mentioned. And the land thus purchased will be no doubt, as far as possible, located in one district of country, which will be settled very differently from the way we now settle up these mountain regions. You may ask, in what respect we shall differ in settling up those countries when we go there to fulfill the commandments of the Lord? I will tell you. No man in those localities will be permitted to receive a stewardship on those lands, unless he is willing to consecrate all his properties to the Lord. That will be among the first teachings given. . . . In that day the whole of our properties, amounting to a very much larger sum, will be held in trust. For whom? For the Church of Jesus Christ of Latter-Saints [*sic*], and for all this great company that will be gathered together (Orson Pratt, JD, Vol. 21:149–50).

We do not wish to leave this land, because it is not fertile, or because it is not a favored land. We appreciate the home that God has given us here, so fruitful in blessings to the Saints; but we look forward to that land with indescribable feelings, because it is the place where God has said His City shall be built (George Q. Cannon, JD, Vol. 11:336–37).

❏ The City of Zion

. . . There are no people now upon the face of the earth, so rich as the Latter-day Saints will be in a few years to come. Having their millions; therefore they will purchase the land, build up cities, towns, and villages, build a great capital city, at headquarters, in Jackson County, Missouri (Orson Pratt, JD, Vol. 21:136).

. . . The cities and temples which we are now engaged in building, we expect to decay; we expect the rock and the various building materials will in time waste away, according to natural laws. But when we build that great central city, the New Jerusalem, there will be so such thing as the word decay associated with it; it will not decay any more than the pot of manna which was gathered by the children of Israel and put into a sacred place in the ark of the covenant. It was preserved from year to year by the power of God; so will he preserve the city of the New Jerusalem, the dwelling houses, the tabernacles, the Temples, etc., from the effects of storms and time (Orson Pratt, JD, Vol. 21:153).

❏ The plan

Through Joseph Smith the Lord gave the plan for the City of Zion and the communities surrounding it. The city plat with 49 blocks will provide for from fifteen to twenty thousand people. The blocks are to be laid off in squares, but the houses will face in alternating directions from block to block. The plan calls for the streets to be 132 feet wide. The farmland will be located outside the city. All homes are to be within six blocks of the center of the city where the Temple and public buildings will be found. Other plats will be set up in surrounding areas as the population increases (see HC Vol. 1, chap. 26).

The plan which he presented was given to him by vision, and the future will prove that the visions of Joseph concerning Jackson County, all the various stakes of Zion and the redemption of Israel will be fulfilled in the time appointed of the Lord (Wilford Woodruff, Journal History, April 6, 1837, Vol. 1:134).

❏ Under the direction of the Lord

We talk of returning to Jackson County to build the most magnificent temple that ever was formed on the earth and the most splendid city that was ever erected; yea, cities, if you please. The architectural designs of those splendid edifices, cities, walls, gardens, bowers, streets, etc, will be under the direction of the Lord, who will control and manage all these matters; and the people, from the President down, will all be under the guidance and direction of the Lord in all the pursuits of human life; until eventually they will be enabled to erect cities that will be fit to be caught up—that when Zion descends from above, Zion will also ascend beneath, and be prepared to associate with those from above (John Taylor, JD, Vol. 10:147).

❏ To be built by a remnant of Jacob assisted by the Gentiles

They [the Gentiles, who come into the Church after the internal strife in America] shall assist my people, the remnant of Jacob, and also as many of the house of Israel as shall come, that they may build a city, which shall be called the New Jerusalem (3 Nephi 21:23).

And that a New Jerusalem should be built up upon this land, unto the remnant of the seed of Joseph out of the land of Jerusalem, that he might be merciful unto the seed of Joseph that they should perish not.

Wherefore, the remnant of the house of Joseph shall be built upon this land; and it shall be a land of their inheritance; and they shall build up a holy city unto the Lord, like unto the Jerusalem of old; and they shall no more be confounded, until the end come when the earth shall pass away (Ether 13:1–9).

My attention has been called to statements in the Book of Mormon which some interpret to mean that the Lamanites will take the lead in building the temple and the New Jerusalem in Missouri. But I fail to find any single passage which indicates that this is to be the order of things when these great events are to be fulfilled.

Most of the passages used as evidence, in an attempt to prove that the Lamanites will take the lead and we are to follow, seem to come from the instruction given by our Lord when He visited the Nephites after his resurrection. Chapters 20 and 21 of Third Nephi are the main sources for this conclusion. But I fail to find in any of the words delivered by our Savior any declaration out of which this conclusion can be reached. It all comes about by a misunderstanding and an improper interpretation.

In these chapters the Lord is speaking throughout of the remnant of Jacob. Who is Jacob whose remnant is to perform this great work in the last days? Most assuredly Jacob is Israel. Then again, when he speaks of the seed of Joseph, who is meant? Those who are descendants of Joseph, son of Israel, and this includes, of course, the Lamanites as well as the Ephramites who are now being assembled and who are taking their place, according to prophecy, at the head to guide and bless the whole house of Israel. . . .

I take it we, the members of the Church, most of us of the tribe of Ephraim, are of the remnant of Jacob. We know it to be the fact that the Lord called upon the descendants of Ephraim to commence his work in the earth in these last days. We know further that he has said that he set Ephraim, according to the promises of his birthright, at the head. Ephraim receives th "richer blessings," these blessings being those of presidency or direction. The keys are with Ephraim. It is Ephraim who is to be endowed with power to bless and give to the other tribes, including the Lamanites, their blessings. All the other tribes of Jacob, including the Lamanites, are to be crowned with glory in Zion by the hand of Ephraim.

Now do the scriptures teach that Ephraim, after doing all of this is to abdicate, or relinquish his place, and give it to the Lamanites and then receive orders from this branch of the "remnant of Jacob" in the building of the New Jerusalem? This certainly is inconsistent with the whole plan and with all that the Lord has revealed in the Doctrine and Covenants in relation to the establishment of Zion and the building of the New Jerusalem. . . .

That the remnants of Joseph, found among the descendants of Lehi will have part in this great work is certainly consistent, and the great work of this restoration, the building of the temple and the City of, or New Jerusalem, will fall to the lot of the descendants of Joseph, but it is Ephraim who will stand at the head and direct the work (Joseph Fielding Smith, *Doctrines of Salvation,*Vol. 2:247–50).

❏ A land of peace

. . . We believe that we shall rear splendid edifices, magnificent temples and beautiful cities that shall become the pride, praise and glory of the whole earth. We believe that this people will excel in literature, in science and the arts and in manufactures. In fact, there will be a concentration of wisdom, not only of the combined wisdom of the world as it now exists, but men will be inspired in regard to all these matters in a manner and to an extent that they never have been before, and we shall have eventually, when the Lord's purposes are carried out, the most magnificent buildings, the most pleasant and beautiful gardens, the richest and most costly clothing and be the most healthy and the most intellectual people that will reside upon the earth. . . . Zion will become the praise of the whole earth. . . . In fact, if there is anything great, noble, dignified, exalted, anything pure, or holy, or virtuous, or lovely, anything calculated to exalt or ennoble the human mind to dignify and elevate the people, it will be found among the people of the Saints of the most High God (John Taylor, JD, Vol. 10:146–47).

And it shall be called the New Jerusalem, a land of peace, a city of refuge, a place of safety for the saints of the Most High God;

And the glory of the Lord shall be there, and the terror of the Lord also shall be there, insomuch that the wicked will not come unto it, and it shall be called Zion.

And it shall come to pass among the wicked, that every man that will not take his sword against his neighbor must needs flee unto Zion for safety.

And there shall be gathered unto it out of every nation under heaven; and it shall be the only people that shall not be at war one with another.

And it shall be said among the wicked: Let us not go up to battle against Zion, for the inhabitants of Zion are terrible; wherefore we cannot stand.

And it shall come to pass that the righteous shall be gathered out from among all nations, and shall come to Zion, singing with songs of everlasting joy (D&C 45:66–71).

❏ A temple will be built

Hearken, O ye Elders of my Church, saith the Lord your God, who have assembled yourselves together, according to my commandments, in this land, which is the land of Missouri, which is the land which I have appointed and consecrated for the gathering of the Saints.

Wherefore, this is the land of promise, and the place for the city of Zion. And thus saith the Lord your God, if you will receive wisdom here is wisdom. Behold, the place which is now called Independence is the Center place; and a spot for the temple is lying westward, upon a lot which is not far from the courthouse. Wherefore, it is wisdom that the land should be purchased by the Saints, and also every tract lying westward, even unto the line running directly between Jew and Gentile (D&C 57:1–5).

. . . I seemed to be standing on the west bank of the Missouri River opposite the City of Independence but I saw no City. I saw the whole States of Missouri Illinois and part of Iowa were a Complete wilderness with no living human being in them. I then saw a short distance from the river Twelve men dressed in the robes of the Temple Standing in a square or nearly so. I understood it represented the Twelve gates of the New Jerusalem, and they were with hands uplifted Consecrating the ground and laying the Corner Stones. I saw myriads of Angels hovering over them and around about them and also an immense pillar of a Clawd over them and I heard the singing of the most beautif[ul] music the words "Now is established the Kingdom of our God and His Christ, and He shall reign forever and Ever, and the Kingdom shall never be Thrown down for the Saints have overcome." And I saw people coming from the river and different places a long way off to help build the Temple, and it seemed that the Hosts of the angels also helped to get the material to build the Temple . . . (*A Remarkable Vision* [see appendix]).

. . . Together you (the Lamanites) and we shall build in the spectacular city of New Jerusalem the temple to which our Redeemer will come. Your hands with ours, also those of Jacob, will place the foundation stones, raise the walls, and roof the magnificent structure. Perhaps your artistic hands will paint the temple and decorate it with a master's touch, and together we shall dedicate to our Creator Lord the most beautiful of all temples ever built in his name (Spencer W. Kimball, IE, December 1959, pp. 938–39).

There, however, we expect to build a temple different from all other temples in some respects. It will be built much larger, cover a larger area of ground, for larger than this Tabernacle covers, and this Tabernacle will accommodate from 12,000 to 15,000 people. We expect to build a temple much larger, very much larger, according to the revelation God gave to us forty years ago in regard to that Temple. But you may ask in what form will it be built? Will it be built in one large room, like this Tabernacle! No; there will be 24 different compartments in the Temple that will be built in Jackson County. The names of these compartments were given to us some forty-five or forty-six years ago; the names we still have, and when we build these twenty-four rooms, in a circular form and arched over the center, we shall give the names to all these different compartments just as the Lord specified through Joseph Smith. . . . Perhaps you may ask for what purpose these twenty-four compartments are to be built. I answer not to assemble the outside world in, nor to assemble the Saints all in one place, but these buildings will be built with a special view to the different orders, or in other words, the different quorums or councils of the two Priesthood that God has ordained on the earth. . . . But will there be any other buildings excepting those 24 rooms that are all joined together in a circular form and arched over the center—are there any other rooms that will be built—detached from the Temple? Yes. There will be tabernacles, there will be meeting houses for the assembling of the people on the Sabbath day. There will be various places of meeting so that the people may gather together; but the Temple will be dedicated to the Priesthood of the Most High God, and for most sacred and holy purposes (Orson Pratt, JD, Vol. 24:24–25).

❏ Jesus will appear

. . . And the Lord Jesus will appear and show Himself unto His servants in His temple in holy places, to counsel and instruct and direct. He will appear in the glory of His Father, in His resurrected body, among those who can endure His presence and glory. And all this I expect long before He will waste away and destroy the wicked from off the face of the earth (Erastus Snow, JD, Vol. 25:34).

Among the first-mentioned of these three classes of men, the Lord will make his appearance first; and that appearance will be unknown to the rest of mankind. He will come to the Temple prepared for him, and his faithful people will behold his face, hear his voice, and gaze upon his glory. From his own lips they will receive further instructions for the development and beautifying of Zion and for the extension and sure stability of his Kingdom (Charles W. Penrose, MS, September 10, 1859).

❏ Freedom of Religion

Those who will not take up their sword to fight against their neighbor must needs flee to Zion for safety. And they will come, saying, we do not know anything of the principles of your religion, but we perceive that you are an honest community; you administer justice and righteousness, and we want to live with you and receive the protection of your laws, but as for your religion we will talk about that some other time. Will we protect such people? Yes, all honorable men. When the peoples shall have torn to shreds the Constitution of the United States the Elders of Israel will be found holding it up to the nations of the earth and proclaiming liberty and equal rights to all men and extending the hand of fellowship to the oppressed of all nations. . . (John Taylor, JD, Vol. 21:8).

When Zion is established in her beauty and honor and glory, the kings and princes of the earth will come, in order that they may get information and teach the same to their people. They will come as they came to learn the wisdom of Solomon (John Taylor, JD, Vol. 6:169).

−13−

❑ ISRAEL WILL BE GATHERED

❑ Who is Israel?

Jacob (the grandson of Abraham) became the father of 12 sons. Through the stewardship of his 11th son, Joseph, the entire family relocated to Egypt to escape a lengthy famine. Sometime after the death of Joseph, a new pharaoh became concerned that the rapidly multiplying Israelites could become allied to Egypt's enemies in the event of a war. His solution was to put them into slavery.

After generations of servitude, the Israelites were miraculously delivered by Moses. . . .

Under the leadership of Moses' successor, Joshua, Israel took possession of most of the land of Canaan. . . . They were located between Egypt and Mesopotamia. . . .

Upon the death of solomon, 10 of the tribes of Israel rebelled against Solomon's son Rehoboam and chose Jeroboam from the tribe of Ephraim as their king. Primarily it was the tribe of Judah and half of the tribe of Benjamin who stayed loyal to the house of David and Solomon. This split resulted in the formation of two distinct nations. The tribes in the north retained the name Israel with the seat of government located in the city of Samaria, while the tribes in the south were designated as the kingdom of Judah with Jerusalem as its capital. . . .

The northern kingdom of Israel was especially resistant to (the warnings of the prophets). Consequently, in about

721 B.C. the Lord allowed Assyria, . . . to invade it and take its tribes captive. . . . There was none left but the tribe [kingdom] of Judah. (2 Kgs. 17:6, 18). The Assyrians placed them in the city of Halah and in the cities of the Medes. . . . Their story there-after is not discussed in biblical text, and thus they became known as the lost tribes of Israel. . . .

In about 587 B.C. the inhabitants of Jerusalem were conquered by Babylon and later became subject to other nations . . . (Paul K. Browning, *Ensign*, July 1998 pp.56–58).

❏ The fate of Judah

. . . Jeremiah prophesied that Judah would serve the Babylonians for 70 years and then be liberated. Ezra records the fulfillment of this prophecy . . . a minority returned to the land of Jerusalem. The rest remained in the communities of what was the Persian empire. Those who returned to jerusalem rebuilt the city and the temple; over the next five centuries their descendants became subjects of Persia, Greece, and finally Rome. . . . Almost 40 years after his (Jesus Christ) Crucifixion, Jews in the holy Land rebelled against the Romans. . . . In A.D. 70 Rome crushed the revolt . . . Jews were dispersed throughout all parts of the Roman world. . . .

The Book of Mormon account of the Lehites and the Mulekites, two groups of Israelites who were dispersed from Jerusalem just before the main Babylonian invasion, is also important in the story of the scattering of Israel.

. . . It is clear that an important component of the latter-day gathering of Israel involves worldwide missionary work. Those who are spiritually ready among the nations hearken to the gospel message . . . (Ibid., pp. 58–60).

❏ The Lost Tribes taken by the Assyrians

. . . Once they were taken by the Assyrians, the historical narrative about them in the Bible comes to an end. However, other sources both scriptural and nonscriptural give limited information regarding their fate (Ibid., p. 59).

They seem to have departed from Assyria, . . . [and] there is abundant evidence that their journey was toward the north. The Lord's word through Jeremiah promises that the people shall be brought back "from the land of the north" [Jeremiah 16:15; 23:8; 31:8], and a similar declaration has been made through divine revelation in the present dispensation [see D&C 133:26–27]. . . .

. . . We find references to the north-bound migration of the Ten Tribes, which they undertook in accordance with a plan to escape the heathen by going to a farther country "where never man dwelt, that they might there keep their statutes which they never kept in their own land" [see 2 Esdras 13:40–45]. The same writer informs us that they journeyed a year and a half into the north country, but he gives us evidence that many remained in the land of their captivity (James E. Talmage, *The Articles of Faith*, p. 325).

But now I go unto the Father, and also to show myself unto the lost tribes of Israel, for they are not lost unto the Father, for he knoweth whither he hath taken them (3 Nephi 17:4).

Many mixed with the people where they were scattered

The Ten Tribes were taken by force out of the land the Lord gave them. Many of them mixed with the peoples among whom they were scattered. A large portion, however, departed in one body into the north and disappeared from the rest of the world. Where they went and where they are we do not know. That they are intact we must believe, else how shall the scripture be fulfilled? There are too many prophecies concerning them and their return in a body for us to ignore the fact (Joseph Fielding Smith, *The Way to Perfection,* p. 130).

❏ The main body departed to the north

And they who are in the north countries shall come in remembrance before the Lord; and their prophets shall hear his voice, and shall no longer stay themselves; and they shall smite the rocks, and the ice shall flow down at their presence.

And an highway shall be cast up in the midst of the great deep. Their enemies shall become a prey unto them,

And in the barren deserts there shall come forth pools of living water; and the parched ground shall no longer be a thirsty land.

And they shall bring forth their rich treasures unto the children of Ephraim, my servants.

And the boundaries of the everlasting hills shall tremble at their presence.

And there shall they fall down and be crowned with glory, even in Zion, by the hands of the servants of the Lord, even the children of Ephraim.

And they shall be filled with songs of everlasting joy (D&C 133:26–33).

❏ Zion will be established before their return

. . . It is plain that, while many of those belonging to the Ten Tribes were diffused among the nations, a sufficient number to justify the retention of the original name were led away as a body and are now in existence in some place where the

88

Lord has hidden them. To them the resurrected Christ went to minister after His visit to the Nephites. Their return constitutes a very important part of the gathering, characteristic of the dispensation of the fulness of times.

From the express and repeated declaration, that in their exodus from the north the Ten Tribes are to be led to Zion, there to receive honor at the hands of those who are of Ephraim, who necessarily are to have previously gathered there, it is plain that Zion is to be first established (James E. Talmage, *The Articles of Faith,* pp. 340–41).

❏ Prophets of the lost tribes

Having spoken concerning the gathering of the ten tribes, I will refer again to their Prophets. "Their Prophets shall hear his voice." Do not think that we are the only people who will have prophets. God is determined to raise up Prophets among that people, but he will not bestow upon them all the fulness of the blessings of the Priesthood. The fulness will be reserved to be given to them after they come to Zion. But Prophets will be among them while in the north, and a portion of the Priesthood will be there; and John the Revelator will be there, teaching, instructing and preparing them for this great work (Orson Pratt, JD, Vol. 18:25).

During the conference of June 2–6, 1831, the Prophet Joseph Smith stated that John the Revelator was at that time laboring among the lost tribes (Joseph Smith, HC, Vol. 1:176).

❏ A history to be kept

For behold, I shall speak unto the Jews and they shall write it; and I shall also speak unto the Nephites and they shall write it; and I shall also speak unto the other tribes of the house of Israel, which I have led away, and they shall write it: and I shall also speak unto all nations of the earth and they shall write it.

And it shall come to pass that the Jews shall have the words of the Nephites, and the Nephites shall have the words of the Jews; and the Nephites and the Jews shall have the words of the lost tribes of Israel; and the lost tribes of Israel shall have the words of the Nephites and the Jews (2 Nephi 29:12–13).

. . . The tribes shall come; they are not lost unto the Lord; they shall be brought forth as hath been predicted; and I say unto you, there are those now living—aye, some here present— who shall live to read the records of the Lost Tribes of Israel, which shall be made one with the record of the Jews, or the Holy Bible, and the record of the Nephites, or the Book of Mormon, even as the Lord hath predicted (James E. Talmage, CR, April 1916, p. 130).

❏ Preparation for their return

. . . Pestilence, hail, famine, and earthquake will sweep the wicked of this generation from off the face of the land, to open and prepare the way for the return of the lost tribes of Israel from the north country (Joseph Smith, HC, Vol. 1:315).

. . . After Zion is built in Jackson County, and after the Temple is built upon that spot of ground where the corner stone was laid in 1831; after the glory of God in the form of a cloud by day shall rest upon that Temple, and by night the shining of a flaming fire will fill the whole heavens round about; after every dwelling place upon Mount Zion shall be clothed upon as with a pillar of fire by night, and a cloud by day, about that period of time, the ten tribes will be heard of, away in the north, a great company, as Jeremiah says, coming down from the northern regions, coming to sing in the height of the latter-day Zion (Orson Pratt, JD, Vol. 18:68).

❏ An inheritance in Palestine

By and by, when all things are prepared—when the Jews have received their scourging, and Jesus has descended upon the Mount of Olives, the ten tribes will leave Zion, and will go to Palestine, to inherit the land that was given to their ancient fathers, and it will be divided amongst the descendants of Abraham, Isaac and Jacob by the inspiration of the Holy Ghost. They will go there to dwell in peace in their own land from that time, until the earth shall pass away. But Zion, after their departure, will still remain upon the western hemisphere, and she will be crowned with glory as well as old Jerusalem, and, as the Psalmist David says, she will become the joy of the whole earth. "Beautiful for situation is Mount Zion on the sides of the north, the city of the great King" (Orson Pratt, JD, Vol. 18:68).

−14−

❏ THE MISSION TO THE JEWS WHEN THE TIME OF THE GENTILES IS FULFILLED

That through your administration they may receive the word, and through their administration the word may go forth unto the ends of the earth, unto the Gentiles first, and then, behold, and lo, they shall turn unto the Jews (D&C 90:9).

The Twelve are a Traveling Presiding High Council, to officiate in the name of the Lord, under the direction of the Presidency of the Church, agreeable to the institution of heaven; to build up the church, and regulate all the affairs of the same in all nations, first unto the Gentiles and secondly unto the Jews (D&C 107:33).

Send forth the elders of my church unto the nations which are afar off; unto the islands of the sea; send forth unto foreign lands; call upon all nations, first upon the Gentiles, and then upon the Jews (D&C 133:8).

And they also of the tribe of Judah, after their pain, shall be sanctified in holiness before the Lord, to dwell in his presence day and night, forever and ever (D&C 133:35).

15

❏ THE LAMANITES WILL BE CONVERTED

And for this very purpose are these plates preserved, which contain these records—that the promises of the Lord might be fulfilled, which he made to his people;

And that the Lamanites might come to a knowledge of their fathers, and that they might know the promises of the Lord, and that they may believe the gospel and rely upon the merits of Jesus Christ, and be glorified through faith in his name, and that through their repentance they might be saved (D&C 3:19–20).

. . . The coming of Christ seems to be near at hand, yet Zion must be redeemed before that day; the temple must be built upon the consecrated spot, the cloud and glory of the Lord rest upon it, and the Lamanites, many of them, brought in, and they must build up the New Jerusalem! It is true, so says the Book of Mormon, that inasmuch as the Gentiles receive the Gospel, they shall assist my people the remnant of Jacob, saith the Lord, to build the New Jerusalem. And when they have got it built, then we are told that they shall assist my people who are of Jacob to be gathered unto the New Jerusalem.

Only a few thousand or hundreds of thousands, then, are to be engaged in this work, and then, after it is done, we are to assist the Lamanites to gather in; and then shall the powers of heaven be in your midst; and then is the coming of Christ.

It will not be before the Lamanites come in, nor before the temple is constructed in Jackson County; but there is a great people to do the work (Orson Pratt, JD, Vol. 3:18).

We also bear testimony that the "Indians" (so-called) of North and South America are a remnant of the tribes of Israel, as is now made manifest by the discovery and revelation of their ancient oracles and records.

The despised and degraded son of the forest, who has wandered in defection and sorrow, and suffered reproach, shall then drop his disguise and stand forth in manly dignity, and exclaim to the Gentiles who have envied and sold him—"I am Joseph; does my father yet live?" or in other words, I am a descendant of that Joseph who was sold into Egypt. You have hated me, and sold me, and thought I was dead; but lo! I live and am heir to the inheritance, titles, honours, priesthood, sceptre, crown, throne, and eternal life and dignity of my fathers, who live for evermore.

He shall then be ordained, washed, anointed with holy oil, and arrayed in fine linen, even the glorious and beautiful garments and royal robes of the high priesthood, which is after the order of the Son of God; and shall enter into the congregation of the Lord, even into the Holy of Holies, there to be crowned with authority and power which shall never end.

The spirit of the Lord shall then descend upon him like the dew upon the mountains of Hermon, and like refreshing showers of rain upon the flowers of Paradise.

His heart shall expand with knowledge, wide as eternity, and his mind shall comprehend the vast creations of his God, and his eternal purpose of redemption, glory, and exaltation, which was devised in heaven before the worlds were organized; but made manifest in these last days, for the fulness of the Gentiles, and for the exaltation of Israel ("Proclamation of the Twelve Apostles of the Church of Jesus Christ of Latter-day Saints," MS, October 22, 1845).

Historians have written about your past; poets have sung of your possibilities; prophets have predicted your scattering and your gathering; and your Lord has permitted you to walk through the dark chasms of your ancestor's making, but has patiently waited for your awakening, and now smiles on your florescence, and points the way to your glorious future as sons and daughters of God. You will arise from your bed of affliction and from your condition of deprivation if you will accept fully the Lord, Jesus Christ, and his total program. You will rise to former heights in culture and education, influence and power. You will blossom as the rose upon the mountains. Your daughters will be nurses, teachers, and social workers, and, above all, beloved wives and full-of-faith mothers of a righteous posterity.

Your sons will compete in art, literature, and medicine, in law, architecture, etc. They will become professional, industrial and business leaders, and statesmen of the first order (Spencer W. Kimball, IE, December 1959, pp. 938–39).

But before the great day of the Lord shall come, Jacob shall flourish in the wilderness, and the Lamanites shall blossom as the rose (D&C 49:24).

16

❏ A UNIVERSAL CONFLICT

But, behold, in the last days, or in the days of the Gentiles—yea, behold all the nations of the Gentiles and also the Jews, both those who shall come upon this land and those who shall be upon other lands, yea, even upon all the lands of the earth, behold, they will be drunken with iniquity and all manner of abominations—

And when that day shall come they shall be visited of the Lord of Hosts, with thunder and with earthquake, and with a great noise, and with storm, and with tempest, and with the flame of devouring fire.

And all the nations that fight against Zion, and that distress her, shall be as a dream of a night vision; yea, it shall be unto them, even as unto a hungry man which dreameth, and behold he eateth but he awaketh and his soul is empty (2 Nephi 27:1–3).

And it shall be called the New Jerusalem, a land of peace, a city of refuge, a place of safety for the saints of the Most High God:

And the glory of the Lord shall be there, and the terror of the Lord also shall be there, insomuch that the wicked will not come unto it, and it shall be called Zion.

And it shall come to pass among the wicked, that every man that will not take his sword against his neighbor must needs flee unto Zion for safety.

And there shall be gathered unto it out of every nation under heaven; and it shall be the only people that shall not be at war one with another (D&C 45:66–69).

. . . And as these judgments come, kingdoms and thrones will be cast down and overturned. Empire will war with empire, kingdom with kingdom, and city with city, and there will be one general revolution throughout the earth, the Jews fleeing to their own country, desolation coming upon the wicked, with the swiftness of whirlwinds and fury poured out (Orson Pratt, JD, Vol. 14:65–66).

. . . By-and-by the Spirit of God will entirely withdraw from those Gentile nations, and leave them to themselves. Then they will find something else to do besides warring against the Saints in their midst—besides raising their sword and fighting against the Lamb of God; for then war will commence in earnest, and such a war as probably never entered into the hearts of men in our age to conceive of. No nation of the Gentiles upon the face of the whole earth but what will be engaged in deadly war, except the Latter-day Kingdom. They will be fighting one against another. And when that day comes, the Jews will flee to Jerusalem, and those nations will almost use one another up, and those of them who are left will be burned; for that will be the last sweeping judgment that is to go over the earth to cleanse it from wickedness (Orson Pratt, JD, Vol. 7:188).

And it came to pass that I beheld that the wrath of God was poured out upon that great and abominable church, insomuch that there were wars and rumors of wars among all the nations and kindreds of the earth (1 Nephi 14:15).

-17-

❏ CALLING OF THE 144,000

And I saw another angel ascending from the east, having the seal of the living God: and he cried with a loud voice to the four angels, to whom it was given to hurt the earth and the sea,

Saying, Hurt not the earth neither the sea, nor the trees, till we have sealed the servants of our God in their foreheads.

And I heard the number of them which were sealed: and there were sealed an hundred and forty and four thousand of all the tribes of the children of Israel (Revelation 7:2–4).

The Prophet Joseph Smith taught that this sealing "signifies sealing the blessing upon their heads, meaning the everlasting covenant, thereby making their calling and election sure" (Joseph Smith, HC, Vol. 5:530).

. . . The Ten Tribes will have to come forth and come to this land, to be crowned with glory in the midst of Zion by the hands of the servants of God, even the children of Ephraim. . . . All that will be done, probably, in the morning of the seventh thousand years (Orson Pratt, JD, Vol. 16:325–26).

I am going on in my progress for eternal life. It is not only necessary that you should be baptized for your dead, but you will have to go through all the ordinances for them the same as you have gone through to save yourselves. There will be 144,000 saviors on Mount Zion, and with them an innumerable host that no man can number. Oh! I beseech you to go forward, go forward and make your calling and your election sure; and if any man preach any other Gospel than that which I have preached, he shall be cursed (Joseph Smith, HC, Vol. 6:365).

What are we to understand by sealing the one hundred and forty-four thousand, out of all the tribes of Israel—twelve thousand out of every tribe?

We are to understand that those who are sealed are high priests, ordained unto the holy order of God, to administer the everlasting gospel; for they are they who are ordained out of every nation, kindred, tongue, and people, by the angels to whom is given power over the nations of the earth, to bring as many as will come to the church of the Firstborn (D&C 77:11–12).

When the Temple is built the sons of the two Priesthood, that is, those who are ordained to the Priesthood of Melchizedec, that Priesthood which is after the order of the Son of God, with all its appendages; and those who have been ordained to the Priesthood of Aaron with all its appendages, the former called the sons of Moses, the latter the sons of Aaron, will enter into that Temple . . . and all of them who are pure in heart will behold the face of the Lord and that too before he comes in his glory in the clouds of heaven, for he will suddenly come to His Temple, and He will purify the sons of Moses and of Aaron, until they shall be prepared to offer in that Temple an offering that shall be acceptable in the sight of the Lord. In doing this, he will purify not only the minds of the Priesthood in that Temple, but he will purify their bodies until they shall be quickened, and renewed and strengthened, and they will be partially changed, not to immortality, but changed in part that they can be filled with the power of God, and they can stand in the presence of Jesus, and behold his face in the midst of that Temple.

This will prepare them for further ministrations among the nations of the earth,—it will prepare them to go forth in the days of tribulation and vengeance upon the nations of the wicked, when God will smite them with pestilence, plague and earthquake, such as former generations never knew. Then the servants of God will need to be armed with the power of God, they will need to have that sealing blessing pronounced upon their foreheads that they can stand forth in the midst of these desolations and plagues and not be overcome by them. When John the Revelator describes this scene he says he saw four angels sent forth, ready to hold the four winds that should blow from the four quarters of heaven. Another angel ascended from the east and cried to the four angels, and said, "Smite not the earth now, but wait a little while." "How long?" "Until the servants of our God are sealed in their foreheads." What for? To prepare them to stand forth in the midst of these desolations and plagues, and not be overcome. When they are prepared, when they have received a renewal of their bodies in the Lord's temple, and have been filled with the Holy Ghost and purified as gold and silver in a furnace of fire, then they will be prepared to stand before the nations of the earth and preach glad tidings of salvation in the midst of judgments that are to come like a whirlwind upon the wicked (Orson Pratt, JD, Vol. 15:365–66).

−18−

❏ PREPARATION FOR THE LORD'S SECOND COMING

❏ Have an unshakable testimony

Unless every member of this Church gains for himself an unshakable testimony of the divinity of this Church, he will be among those who will be deceived in this day when the "elect according to the covenant" are going to be tried and tested. Only those will survive who have gained for themselves this testimony (Harold B. Lee, CR, October, 1950, p. 129).

❏ Seek not to hasten the Lord's work

Are you prepared for the day of vengeance, to come, when the Lord will consume the wicked by the brightness of his coming? No. Then do not be too anxious for the Lord to hasten his work. Let our anxiety be centered upon this one thing, the sanctification of our hearts, the purifying of our own affections, the preparing of ourselves for the approach of the events that are hastening upon us. This should be our daily prayer, and not to be in a hurry to see the overthrow of the wicked. . . . Seek not to hasten it, but be satisfied to let the Lord have his own time and way, and be patient. Seek to have the Spirit of Christ, that we may wait patiently the time of the Lord, and prepare ourselves for the times that are coming. This is our duty (Brigham Young, DEN, May 1, 1861, p. 1).

❏ Know God and His Son

Now, I have asked myself, this being the time to prepare for the millennial reign, how shall we set about to prepare a people to receive the coming of the Lord? As I have thought seriously about that matter, I have reached two or three sure conclusions in my own thinking. This preparation demands first that a people, to receive the coming of the Lord, must be taught the personality and the nature of God and his Son, Jesus Christ. . . .

To my thinking, another requisite of that preparation to receive the Lord at the beginning of his millennial reign demands that the people be taught to accept the divinity of the mission of Jesus as the Savior of the world (Harold B. Lee, CR, October, 1956, pp. 61–62).

❏ Be clean and pure

[There is] still another requirement, as I see it, for a people to be prepared to receive the Savior's coming. We must be cleansed and purified and sanctified to be made worthy to receive and abide that holy presence (Ibid.).

❏ Accept Joseph Smith

And now, finally, there is still one thing more that is necessary, to my thinking, before that preparation is made for the millennial reign. We must accept the divine mission of the Prophet Joseph Smith as the instrumentality through which the restoration of the gospel and the organization of the Church of Jesus Christ was accomplished (Ibid.).

❏ Follow the Prophet

Now the only safety we have as members of this Church is to do exactly what the Lord said to the Church in that day when the Church was organized. We must learn to give heed to the words and commandments that the Lord shall give through his prophet, "as he receiveth them, walking in all holiness before me; . . . as if from mine own mouth, in all patience and faith." (D&C 21:4–5) There will be some things that take patience and faith. You may not like what comes from the authority of the Church. It may contradict your political views. It may contradict your social views. It may interfere with some of your social life. But if you listen to these things, as if from the mouth of the Lord himself, with patience and faith, the promise is that "the gates of hell shall not prevail against you; yea, and the Lord God will disperse the powers of darkness from before you, and cause the heavens to shake for your good, and his name's glory." (D&C 21:6) (Harold B. Lee, IE, December 1970, p. 126).

−19−

❏ EVENTS SOON BEFORE
CHRIST'S COMING IN GLORY

Whoever will look to the words of the Prophets, and to the sayings of Jesus Christ, on this subject, the same will be convinced that all the signs of which I have spoken are clearly pointed out as the signs of His coming. But, notwithstanding all these things are written, His coming will overtake the world unawares, as the flood did the people in the days of Noah. The reason is, they will not understand the Prophets. They will not endure sound doctrine; their ears are turned away from the truth and turned to fables because of false teachers, and the precepts of men . . . (Parley P. Pratt, *A Voice of Warning,* p. 46).

❏ No one knows the day and the time

But of that day and hour knoweth no man, no, not the angels of heaven, but my Father only (Matthew 24:36).

Jesus Christ never did reveal to any man the precise time that He would come. Go and read the Scriptures, and you cannot find anything that specifies the exact hour He would come: and all that say so are false teachers (Joseph Smith, DHC, Vol. 6:254, March 10, 1844).

. . . Of the day and the hour of the coming of Christ no man knoweth. It is not yet, neither is it far off; there are prophecies yet to be fulfilled before that event takes place; therefore, let no man deceive the saints with vain philosophy and false prophecy; for false prophets will arise, and deceive the wicked, and, if possible the good; but while the wicked fear and tremble at surrounding judgments, the Saints will watch and pray; and, waiting the final event in patience, will look calmly on the passing scenery of a corrupted world, and view transpiring events as confirmation of their faith in the holy gospel which they profess, and rejoice more and more, as multiplied signs shall confirm the approach of the millennial day ("Fifth General Epistle of the Presidency of the Church," issued April 7, 1851, found in MS, Vol. 13:210, July 15, 1851).

❑ The surface of the earth changed

. . . And the earth shall tremble, and reel to and fro, and the heavens also shall shake (D&C 45:48).

And every island fled away, and the mountains were not found (Revelation 16:20).

Every valley shall be filled, and every mountain and hill shall be brought low; and the crooked shall be made straight, and the rough ways shall be made smooth (Luke 3–5).

❑ Wonders in the heavens and earth

And I will shew wonders in the heavens and in the earth, blood, and fire, and pillars of smoke.
The sun shall be turned into darkness, and the moon into blood, before the great and the terrible day of the Lord come (Joel 2:30–31).

But, behold, I say unto you that before this great day shall come the sun shall be darkened, and the moon shall be turned into blood, and the stars shall fall from heaven, and there shall be greater signs in heaven above and in the earth beneath (D&C 29:14).

But before that great day shall come, the sun shall be darkened, and the moon be turned into blood; and the stars shall refuse their shining, and some shall fall, and great destructions await the wicked (D&C 34:8).

❏ The sign of Christ will be seen

. . . Then will appear one grand sign of the Son of Man in heaven. But what will the world do? They will say it is a planet, a comet, etc. But the Son of Man will come (even) as the sign of the coming of the Son of Man, which will be as the light of the morning cometh out of the east (*Teachings of the Prophet Joseph Smith,* p. 287).

After the angels have sounded this (their trumps) in the ears of all living, we are informed that there will be a great sign in the heavens. It is not to be limited so that some few only of the human family can see it; but it is said, "All people shall see it together"!" At least, it is to be like our sun seen over one entire side of the globe, and then passing immediately round to the other, or else it will encircle the whole earth at the same time. But the bridegroom does not come then. These are only the preceding events to let the Latter-day Saints and the pure in heart know that these are the times that they may trim up their lamps and prepare for the triumphant appearing of their Lord.

After those angels that I have alluded to have flown through the heavens, this sign is made manifest; and what next? Seven angels are appointed to give their signs and testimonies to the truth of this proclamation of the Gospel, the

Latter-day Saints having previously given theirs. Thus we have the former angels sounding their trumpets, then the great sign, and then comes the seven angels. The first proclaims that great Babylon is about to fall, and her influence to be destroyed. He proclaims that all who remain in Babylon are bound in bundles and their bands made strong, so that no man can unloose them, and that they are therefore prepared for the burning (Orson Pratt, Discourse delivered in the Tabernacle, Salt Lake City, April 8, 1860).

❑ Silence in heaven for the space of half an hour

And when he had opened the seventh seal, there was silence in heaven about the space of half an hour (Revelation 8:1).

And there shall be silence in heaven for the space of half an hour; and immediately after shall the curtain of heaven be unfolded, as a scroll is unfolded after it is rolled up, and the face of the Lord shall be unveiled (D&C 88:95).

20

❏ CHRIST COMES IN GLORY

❏ The earth will be changed to a terrestrial sphere

The earth underwent a baptism by being immersed in water, for the remission of its sins, the washing away of its iniquities. "As it was in the days of Noah, so shall it be in the days of the coming of the Son of Man." Is the world to be deluged in water again? No; because God gave a promise to Noah and set his bow in the clouds as a sign that the world should never again be drowned in water; but in the day of the coming of the Son of Man it will receive the baptism of fire and of the Holy Ghost. John the Baptist said: "There cometh one mightier than I, after me, the latchet of whose shoes I am not worthy to stoop down and unloose. I indeed have baptized you with water: he shall baptize you with the Holy Ghost and with fire." Not only man, but the earth itself, which is a living creature, must undergo this ordinance—this dual baptism (Orson F. Whitney, JD, Vol. 26:266).

He shall command the great deep, and it shall be driven back into the north countries, and the islands shall become one land (D&C 133:23–24).

. . . And every mountain and island were moved out of their places (Revelation 6:14).

For, behold, the Lord cometh forth out of his place, and

will come down, and tread upon the high places of the earth (Micah 1:3).

❏ The Savior revealed

Then, after the wicked begin to recover and get a little strength [from hearing the trumps and seeing the sign], behold and lo! the curtain of heaven will be unfolded as a scroll that is rolled up. You know how our great maps are rolled out to expose their contents to the people; and the Lord has said the heavens shall be unfolded as a scroll that is rolled up is unfolded. What will be seen when this takes place? Our Saviour, our Redeemer, will unvail his face. That Being who was born in Bethlehem—that being who has saved the world by offering his own life, how will he appear? Will he come as a common man? or how will he make his appearance? He will appear as a being whose splendour and glory will cause the sun to hide his face with shame (Orson Pratt, JD, Vol. 8:49–52).

For the Lord himself shall descend from heaven with a shout, with the voice of the archangel, and with the trump of God: and the dead in Christ shall rise first:
Then we which are alive and remain shall be caught up together with them in the clouds, to meet the Lord in the air: and so shall we ever be with the Lord (1 Thessalonians 4:16–17).

Behold, he cometh with clouds; and every eye shall see him, and they also which pierced him: and all kindreds of the earth shall wail because of him (Revelation 1:7).

❏ The wicked will be burned

The mountains quake at him, and the hills melt, and the earth is burned at his presence, yea, the world, and all that dwell therein (Nahum 1:5).

Therefore the inhabitants of the earth are burned, and few men left (Isaiah 24:6).

For behold, saith the prophet, the time cometh speedily that Satan whall have no more power over the hearts of the children of men; for the day soon cometh that all the proud and they who do wickedly shall be as stubble; and the day cometh that they must be burned (1 Nephi 22:15).

He comes! The earth shakes, and the tall mountains tremble; the mighty deep rolls back to the north as in fear, and the rent skies glow like molten brass. He comes! The dead saints burst forth from their tombs, and "those who are alive and remain" are "caught up" with them to meet him. The ungodly rush to hide themselves from his presence and call upon the quivering rocks to cover them. He comes! with all the hosts of the righteous glorified. The breath of his lips strikes death to the wicked. His glory is a consuming fire. The proud and rebellious are as stubble; they are burned and "left neither root nor branch." He sweeps the earth "as with the besom of destruction.'" He deluges the earth with the fiery floods of his wrath, and the filthiness and abominations of the world are consumed. Satan and his dark hosts are taken and bound—the prince of the power of the air has lost his dominion, for he whose right it is to reign has come, and the "kingdoms of this world have become the kingdoms of our Lord and of his Christ" (Charles W. Penrose, MS, September 10, 1859).

And it shall be said: Who is this that cometh down from God in heaven with dyed garments; yea, from the regions which are not known, clothed in his glorious apparel, traveling in the greatness of his strength?

And he shall say: I am he who spake in righteousness, mighty to save.

And the Lord shall be red in his apparel, and his garments like him that treadeth in the wine-vat.

And so great shall be the glory of his presence that the sun shall hide his face in shame, and the moon shall withhold its light, and the stars shall be hurled from their place.

And his voice shall be heard: I have trodden the wine-press alone, and have brought judgment upon all people; and none were with me;

And I have trampled them in my fury, and I did tread upon them in mine anger, and their blood have I sprinkled upon my garments, and stained all my raiment; for this was the day of vengeance which was in my heart (D&C 133:46–51).

❑ Who will be with the Savior when he comes?

And Enoch also, the seventh from Adam, prophesied of these, saying, Behold, the Lord cometh with ten thousands of his saints (Jude 1:14).

Who will be with Jesus when he appears? The decree has gone forth, saying, Mine Apostles who were with me in Jerusalem shall be clothed in glory and be with me. The brightness of their countenance will shine forth with all that effulgence and fulness of splendour that shall surround the Son of Man when he appears. There will be all those personages to whom he alludes. There will be all the former-day Saints, Enoch and his city, with all the greatness and splendour that surround them (Orson Pratt, JD, Vol. 8:51).

21

❏ THE RETURN OF THE CITY OF ENOCH

Enoch was twenty-five years old when he was ordained under the hand of Adam; and he was sixty-five and Adam blessed him.

And he saw the Lord, and he walked with him, and was before his face continually; and he walked with God three hundred and sixty-five years, making him four hundred and thirty years old when he was translated (D&C 107:48–49).

And the Lord called his people Zion, because they were of one heart and one mind, and dwelt in righteousness; and there was no poor among them.

And Enoch continued his preaching in righteousness unto the people of God. and it came to pass in his days, that he built a city that was called the City of Holiness, even Zion (Moses 7:18–19).

And it came to pass that the Lord showed unto Enoch all the inhabitants of the earth; and he beheld, and lo, Zion, in process of time, was taken up into heaven. And the Lord said unto Enoch: Behold mine abode forever (Moses 7:21).

I am the same which have taken the Zion of Enoch into mine own bosom (D&C 38:4).

And all the days of Zion, in the days of Enoch, were three hundred and sixty-five years.

And Enoch and all his people walked with God, and he dwelt in the midst of Zion; and it came to pass that Zion was not, for God received it up into his own bosom; and from thence went forth the saying, Zion is fled (Moses 7:68–69).

. . . He (Enoch) is a ministering angel, to minister to those who shall be heirs of salvation, and appeared unto Jude as Abel did unto Paul; therefore Jude spoke of him (14, 15 verses). And Enoch, the seventh from Adam, revealed these sayings: "Behold, the Lord cometh with ten thousand of His Saints."

Paul was also acquainted with this character, and received instructions from him. (Hebrews 11:5–6) (*Teachings of the Prophet Joseph Smith*, p. 170).

. . . He (the Lord) selected Enoch, whom He directed, and gave His law unto, and to the people who were with him; and when the world in general would not obey the commands of God, after walking with God, he translated Enoch and his church, and the Priesthood or government of heaven was taken away (Ibid., p. 251).

And righteousness will I send down out of heaven; and truth will I send forth out of the earth, to bear testimony of mine Only Begotten; his resurrection from the dead; yea, and also the resurrection of all men; and righteousness and truth will I cause to sweep the earth as with a flood, to gather out mine elect from the four quarters of the earth, unto a place which I shall prepare, an Holy city, that my people may gird up their loins, and be looking forth for the time of my coming; for there shall be my tabernacle, and it shall be called Zion, a New Jerusalem.

And the Lord said unto Enoch: Then shalt thou and all thy city meet them there, and we will receive them into our bosom, and they shall see us; and we will fall upon their necks, and they shall fall upon our necks, and we will kiss each other;

And there shall be mine abode, and it shall be Zion, which shall come forth out of all the creations which I have made; and for the space of a thousand years the earth shall rest (Moses 7:62–64).

. . . By and by when the time came for the accomplishment of the purposes of god, and before the destruction of the wicked, Enoch was caught up to heaven and his Zion with him. and we are told in latter revelation in relation to these matters that a Zion will be built up in our day; that great trouble will overtake the inhabitants of the earth; and that when the time arrives, the Zion that was caught up will descend, and the Zion that will be organized here will ascend, both possessed of the same spirit, their peoples having been preserved by the power of God according to His purposes and as His children, to take part in the events of the latter days. We are told that when the people of these two Zions meet, they will fall on each others' necks, and embrace and kiss each other (John Taylor, JD, Vol. 25:305).

. . . We expect that the Zion which was built up by Enoch, that had no poor in it, will come down again at the commencement of the Millennium to meet the Zion here, according to the song in the Book of Covenants . . . and they shall gaze upon each other's countenances, and see eye to eye (Orson Pratt, JD, Vol. 2:103).

22

❑ THE FIRST RESURRECTION

But before the arm of the Lord shall fall, an angel shall sound his trump, and the saints that have slept shall come forth to meet me in the cloud (D&C 45:45).

And the saints that are upon the earth, who are alive, shall be quickened and be caught up to meet him.
And they who have slept in their graves shall come forth, for their graves shall be opened; and they also shall be caught up to meet him in the midst of the pillar of heaven (D&C 88:96–97).

In modern revelation given to the Church, the Lord had made known more in relation to this glorious event. There shall be at least two classes which shall have the privilege of the resurrection at this time: First those who "shall dwell in the presence of God and his Christ forever and ever"; and second, honorable men, those who belong to the terrestrial kingdom as well as those of the celestial kingdom.

At the time of the coming of Christ, "They who have slept in their graves shall come forth, for their graves shall be opened; and they also shall be caught up to meet him in the midst of the pillar of heaven—They are Christ's, the first fruits, they who shall descend with him first, and they who are on the earth and in their graves, who are first caught up to meet him; and all this by the voice of the sounding of the trump of the angel of God." These are the just, "whose names are written in heaven, where God and Christ are the judge of all. These are they who are just men made perfect through Jesus the Mediator of the new covenant, who wrought out this perfect atonement through the shedding of his own blood" (Joseph Fielding Smith, *Doctrines of Salvation*, Vol. 2:296–98).

❏ Those who are worthy

Following this great event, and after the Lord and the righteous who are caught up to meet him have descended upon the earth, there will come to pass another resurrection. This may be considered as a part of the first, although it comes later. In this resurrection will come forth those of the terrestrial order, who were not worthy to be caught up to meet him, but who are worthy to come forth to enjoy the millennial reign.

It is written that the second angel shall sound, which is the second trump, "and then cometh the redemption of those who are Christ's at his coming; who have received their part in the prison which is prepared for them, that they might receive the gospel, and be judged according to men in the flesh."

This other class, which will also have right to the first resurrection, are those who are not members of the Church of the First Born, but who have led honorable lives, although they refused to accept the fulness of the gospel.

Also in this class will be numbered those who died without law and hence are not under condemnation for a violation of the commandments of the Lord. The promise is made to them of redemption from death in the following words: "And then shall the heathen nations be redeemed, and they that knew no law shall have part in the first resurrection; and it shall be tolerable for them." These, too, shall partake of the mercies of the Lord and shall receive the reuniting of spirit and body inseparably, thus becoming immortal, but not with the fulness of the glory of God (Ibid.).

❏ Those under condemnation must wait

All liars, and sorcerers, and adulterers and all who love and make a lie, shall not receive the resurrection at this time, but for a thousand years shall be thrust down into hell where they shall suffer the wrath of God until they pay the price of their sinning, if it is possible, by the things which they shall suffer.

These are the "spirits of men who are to be judged, and are found under condemnation; And these are the rest of the dead; and they live not again until the thousand years are ended, neither again, until the end of the earth."

These are the hosts of the telestial world who are condemned to "suffer the wrath of God on earth"; and who are the fulness of times, when Christ shall have subdued all enemies under his feet, and shall have perfected his work" (Ibid.).

−23−

❏ THE MILLENNIUM

❏ Christ will reign

The earth hath travailed and brought forth her strength;
And truth is established in her bowels;
And the heavens have smiled upon her;
And she is clothed with the glory of her God;
For he stands in the midst of his people (D&C 84:101).

And also the Lord shall have power over his saints, and shall reign in their midst (D&C 1:36).

For in mine own due time will I come upon the earth in judgment, and my people shall be redeemed and shall reign with me on earth (D&C 43:29).

And there shall be mine abode, and it shall be Zion, which shall come forth out of all the creations which I have made; and for the space of a thousand years the earth shall rest (Moses 7:64).

❏ Satan to be bound

And because of the righteousness of his people, Satan has no power; wherefore, he cannot be loosed for the space of many years; for he hath no power over the hearts of the people, for they dwell in righteousness, and the Holy One of Israel reigneth (1 Nephi 22:26).

And I saw an angel come down from heaven, having the key of the bottomless pit and a great chain in his hand.
And he laid hold on the dragon, that old serpent, which is the Devil, and Satan, and bound him a thousand years.
And cast him into the bottomless pit, and shut him up, and set a seal upon him, that he should deceive the nations no more, till the thousand years should be fulfilled: and after that he must be loosed a little season (Revelation 20:1–3).

For Satan shall be bound, and when he is loosed again he shall only reign for a little season, and then cometh the end of the earth (D&C 43:31).

. . . And Satan shall be bound, that old serpent, who is called the devil, and shall not be loosed for the space of a thousand years. And then he shall be loosed for a little season, that he may gather together his armies (D&C 88:110).

❏ There will be no death

. . . And there shall be no sorrow because there is no death (D&C 101:29).

Wherefore, children shall grow up until they become old; old men shall die; but they shall not sleep in the dust, but they shall be changed in the twinkling of an eye (D&C 63:51).

They shall build, and another shall not inherit it; they shall plant vineyards, and they shall eat the fruit thereof (D&C 101:101).

❏ A pure language

For then will I turn to the people a pure language, that they may all call upon the name of the Lord, to serve him with one consent (Zephaniah 3:9).

❏ The righteous to reign with Christ

And I saw the souls of them that were beheaded for the witness of Jesus, and for the word of God, and which had not worshipped the beast, neither his image, neither had received his mark upon their foreheads, or in their hands; and they lived and reigned with Christ a thousand years (Revelation 20:4).

❏ All things will be revealed

And with righteousness shall the Lord God judge the poor, and reprove with equity for the meek of the earth. . . . And then shall the wolf dwell with the lamb; and the leopard shall lie down with the kid, and the calf, and the young lion, and the fatling, together; and a little child shall lead them. . . . There is nothing which is secret save it shall be revealed; there is no work of darkness save it shall be made manifest in the light; and there is nothing which is sealed upon the earth save it shall be loosed (2 Nephi 30:9–17).

Yea, verily I say unto you, in that day when the Lord shall come, he shall reveal all things—
Things which have passed, and hidden things which no man knew, things of the earth, by which it was made, and the purpose and the end thereof—
Things most precious, things that are above, and things that are beneath, things that are in the earth, and upon the earth, and in heaven (D&C 101:32–34).

❏ Resurrected beings to mingle with mortals

. . . Kings and priests will come here to reign, and will mingle freely among their children of whom they are ancestors. And those who are mortal can receive instruction from those who are immortal, that will prepare them for the time when the earth is to undergo a still greater change. The children of mortality will need this preparation in order to live when theis earth is burning up, which is to be its final destiny (Orson Pratt, JD, Vol. 18:320).

Christ and the resurrected Saints will reign over the earth during the thousand years. They probably will not dwell upon the earth, but will visit it when they please or when it is necessary to govern it (Joseph Smith, HC, Vol. 5:212).

❏ Not everyone will accept the gospel of Jesus Christ

The saying that there will be wicked men on the earth during the Millennium has been misunderstood by many, because the Lord declared that the wicked shall not stand, but shall be consumed. In using this term "wicked" it should be interpreted in the language of the Lord as recorded in the Doctrine and Covenants, section 84, versus 49–53. Here the Lord speaks of those who have not received the gospel as being wicked as they are still under the bondage of sin, having not been baptized. The inhabitants of the terrestrial order will remain on the earth during the Millennium, and this class is without the gospel ordinances (Joseph Fielding Smith, *Doctrines of Salvation,* Vol. 3:63–64).

. . . The Lord will not destroy the agency of the people during the Millennium, therefore there will be a possibility of their sinning during that time. but if they who live then do sin, it will not be because of the power of the devil to tempt them, for he will have no power over them, and they will sin merely because they choose to do so of their own free will (Orson Pratt, JD, Vol. 16:319–20).

When the nations shall see the glory of God together, the spirit of their feelings may be couched in these words, "I will be damned if I will serve you." In those days the Methodists and Presbyterians, headed by their priests, will not be allowed to form into a mob to drive, kill, and rob the Latter-day Saints; neither will the Latter-day Saints be allowed to rise up and say, "We will kill you Methodists, Presbyterians, etc.," neither will any of the different sects of Christendom be allowed to perse-cute each other.

What will they do? They will hear of the wisdom of Zion, and the kings and potentates of the nations will come up to Zion to inquire after the ways of the Lord, and to seek out the great knowledge, wisdom, and understanding manifested through the Saints of the Most High. They will inform the people of God that they belong to such and such a Church, and do not wish to change their religion.

They will be drawn to Zion by the great wisdom displayed there, and will attribute it to the cunning and craftiness of men. It will be asked, "What do you want to do, ye strangers from afar." "We want to live our own religion." "Will you bow the knee before God with us?" O Yes, we would as soon do it as not;" and at that time every knee shall bow, and every tongue acknowledge that God who is the framer and maker of all things, the governor and controller of the universe. They will have to bow the knee and confess that He is God, and that Jesus Christ, who suffered for the sins of the world is actually its Redeemer; that by the shedding of his blood he has redeemed men, women, children, beasts, birds, fish, the earth itself, and everything that John saw and heard praising in heaven (Brigham Young, JD, Vol. 2:316–17).

I most assuredly expect that the time will come when every tongue shall confess, and every knee shall bow, to the Savior, though the people may believe what they will with regard to religion. The kingdom that Daniel saw will actuall make laws to protect every man in his rights, as our government does now, whether the religions of the people are true or false (Brigham Young, JD, Vol. 2:189).

The gospel will be taught far more intensely and with greater power during the millennium, until all the inhabitants of the earth shall embrace it. Satan shall be bound so that he cannot tempt any man. Should any man refuse to repent and accept the gospel under those conditions then he would be accursed. Through the revelations given to the prophets, we learn that during the reign of Jesus Christ for a thousand years eventually all people will embrace the truth. . . . If the knowledge of the Lord covers the earth as the waters do the sea, then it must be universally received. Moreover, the promise of the Lord through Jeremiah is that it will no longer be necessary for anyone to teach his neighbor, "saying, Know the Lord: for they shall all know me, from the least of them unto the greatest of them, saith the Lord" (Joseph Fielding Smith, *Doctrines of Salvation,* Vol. 3:64–65).

. . . The Millennium consists in this—every heart in the church and Kingdom of God being united in one; the Kingdom increasing to the overcoming of everything opposed to the economy of heaven, and Satan being bound, and having a seal set upon him. All things else will be as they are now, we shall eat, drink, and wear clothing. Let the people be holy, and the earth under their feet will be holy (Brigham Young, JD, Vol. 1:203).

❏ Animals to speak

. . . The knowledge of God will cover the whole earth, as the waters cover the great deep. And then the animal creation will manifest more intelligence and more knowledge than they do now, in their fallen condition. Indeed, we have a declaration, by John the Revelator, that when this time shall come, they will even know how to praise God. What? The animal creation endowed with language? Yes, a language of praise, saying something concerning the Lamb that was slain, and about his glory and excellency. What a beautiful creation this will be when all these things are fulfilled (Orson Pratt, JD, Vol. 20:18).

❏ The twelve apostles will

. . . And Jesus and the Twelve Apostles will be in our midst. And we have an account of their thrones. "And Jesus said unto them, Verily, I say unto you, that ye which have followed me, in the regeneration when the Son of Man shall sit in the throne of his glory, ye also shall sit upon twelve thrones, judging the twelve tribes of Israel." Then the twelve tribes will come back, and twelve men sitting on twelve thrones, in the land of Palestine, will reign over them. The Twelve disciples raised up in this land, 1800 years ago, are to have their thrones: who, after being judged themselves by the Twelve at Jerusalem, will sit upon their thrones and will judge the remnant of the tribe of Joseph. And they will have that work to do in the eternal worlds (Orson Pratt, JD, Vol. 19:176).

❏ Temple work

. . . When the Savior comes, a thousand years will be devoted to this work of redemption; and Temples will appear all over this land of Joseph, North and South America and also in Europe and elsewhere (Wilford Woodruff, JD, Vol. 19:230).

The morning of the resurrection dawns upon us. Ere long we will find Joseph and his brethren overseeing and directing the labors of the Elders of Israel in the Temples of our God, laboring for the redemption of the dead, which work will continue during the thousand years rest when the Savior will bear rule over the whole earth (Erastus Snow, JD, Vol. 23:188).

❏ A thousand years of rest

And there shall be mine abode, and it shall be Zion, which shall come forth out of all the creations which I have made; and for the space of a thousand years the earth shall rest (Moses 7:64).

−24−

❏ SATAN WILL BE LOOSED

And when the thousand years are expired, Satan shall be loosed out of his prison,

And shall go out to deceive the nations which are in the four quarters of the earth, Gog and Magog, to gather them together to battle: the number of whom is as the sands of the sea (Revelation 20:7–8).

The battle of Gog and Magog will be after the millennium (Joseph Smith, HC, Vol. 5:298).

. . . I also believe that when Satan is loosed again for a little while, when the thousand years shall be ended, it will be through mankind departing from the practice of those principles which God has revealed, and this Order of Enoch probably among the rest. He can, in no better way, obtain power over the hearts of the children of men, than by appealing to their cupidity, avarice, and low, selfish desires. This is a fruitful cause of difficulty (George Q. Cannon, JD, Vol. 16:119–20).

. . . Thus generation after generation will pass away, during the Millennium, but by and by, at the close of that period, unnumbered millions of the posterity of those who lived during the Millennium will be scattered in the four quarters of the earth, and Satan will be loosed, and will go forth and tempt them, and overcome some of them, so that they will rebel against God; not rebel in ignorance or dwindle in unbelief, as the Lamanites did; but they will sin wilfully against the law of heaven, and so great will the power of Satan be over them, that he will gather them together against the Saints and against the beloved city, and fire will come down out of heaven and consume them (Orson Pratt, JD, Vol. 16:322).

And Michael, the seventh angel, even the archangel, shall gather together his armies, even the hosts of heaven.
And the devil shall gather together his armies; even the hosts of hell, and shall come up to battle against Michael and his armies (D&C 88:112–13).

. . . The Saints then, will have become very numerous, probably more numerous than ever before; and they will be obliged to gather together in one place, as we now do from the four quarters of the earth. They will have to pitch their camps round about, for the "beloved city" will not be large enough for them. . . . Satan will gather his army, consisting of all those angels that fell and left the courts of heaven, when he did, besides all those that will apostatize from the truth, at the end of the thousand years. . . . He with his army will come against the Saints, and the beloved city, and encompass them round about. His army will be so great that it will be able to come upon the Saints on all sides: he is to encompass their camp. . . . He doubtless believes that he will get the mastery and subdue the earth and possess it. I do not think he fully understands all about the designs of God (Orson Pratt, JD, Vol. 18:345–46).

And then cometh the battle of the great God; and the devil and his armies shall be cast away into their own place, that they shall not have power over the saints any more at all.

For Michael (Adam) shall fight their battles, and shall overcome him who seeketh the throne of him who sitteth upon the throne, even the Lamb.

This is the glory of God, and the sanctified; and they shall not any more see death (D&C 88:114–16).

❏ THE EARTH WILL BE DESTROYED

And again, verily, verily, I say unto you that when the thousand years are ended, and men again begin to obey their God, then will I spare the earth but for a little season;

And the end shall come, and the heaven and the earth shall be consumed and pass away, and there shall be a new heaven and a new earth (D&C 29:22–23).

. . . Then, after the holy city and the New Jerusalem are taken np [*sic*] to heaven, the earth will flee away from before the presence of him who sits upon the throne. The earth itself is to pass through a similar change to that which we have to pass through. As our bodies return again to mother dust, forming constituent portions thereof, and no place is found for them as organized bodies, so it will be with this earth. Not only will the elements melt with fervent heat, but the great globe itself will pass away. It will cease to exist as an organized world. It will cease to exist as one of the worlds that are capable of being inhabited. Fire devours all things, converting the earth into its original elements; it passes away into space.

But not one particle of the elements which compose the earth will be destroyed or annihilated. They will all exist and be brought together again by a greater organizing power than is known to man. The earth must be resurrected again, as well as our bodies; its elements will be reunited, and they will be brought together by the power of God's word. He will then so organize these elements now constituted upon this earth, that there will be no curse attached to any of its compound thus made. Now death is connected with them, but then everything will be organized in the most perfect order, just the same as it was when the Lord first formed it (Orson Pratt, JD, Vol. 18:346–47).

–26–

❏ THE FINAL JUDGMENT

And I saw a great white throne, and him that sat on it, from whose face the earth and the heaven fled away; and there was found no place for them.

And I saw the dead, small and great, stand before God; and the books were opened: and another book was opened, which is the book of life: and the dead were judged out of those things which were written in the books, according to their works.

And the sea gave up the dead which were in it; and death and hell delivered up the dead which were in them: and they were judged, every man, according to their works (Revelation 20:11–15).

Then after Satan's army is devoured, and after Satan is cast into hell, and all over whom he has power—then all the inhabitants of the earth will be judged; this great white throne that I have been reading about, will appear; the great and final judgment will come; and when this white throne appears, the earth itself and the literal, temporal heavens that are overhead will flee away, and there will be found no place for them (Orson Pratt, JD, Vol. 18:321).

I am Alpha and Omega, Christ the Lord; yea, even I am he, the beginning and the end, the Redeemer of the world.

I, having accomplished and finished the will of him whose I am, even the Father, concerning me—having done this that I might subdue all things unto myself—

Retaining all power, even to the destroying of Satan and his works at the end of the world, and the last great day of judgment, which I shall pass upon the inhabitants thereof, judging every man according to his works and the deeds which he hath done (D&C 19:1–3).

Wherefore, we shall have a perfect knowledge of all our guilt, and our uncleanness, and our nakedness; and the righteous shall have a perfect knowledge of their enjoyment, and their righteousness, being clothed with purity, yea, even with the robe of righteousness.

And it shall come to pass that when all men shall have passed from this first death unto life, insomuch as they have become immortal, they must appear before the judgment-seat of the Holy One of Israel; and then cometh the judgment, and then must they be judged according to the holy judgment of God (2 Nephi 9:13–16).

And he that receiveth my Father receiveth my Father's kingdom; therefore all that my Father hath shall be given unto him (D&C 84:33–39).

This brings to my mind the vision that Joseph Smith had, when he saw Adam open the gate of the Celestial city and admit the people one by one. He then saw Father Adam conduct them to the throne one by one, where they were crowned Kings and Priests of God (Heber C. Kimball, JD, Vol. 9:41).

When shall we receive our inheritances so that we can say they are our own? When the Savior has completed the work, when the faithful Saints have preached the Gospel to the last of the spirits who have lived here and who are designed to come to this earth; when the thousand years of rest shall come and thousands and thousands of Temples shall be built, and the servants and handmaids of the Lord shall have entered therein and officiated for themselves, and for their dead friends back to the days of Adam; when the last of the spirits in prison who will receive the Gospel has received it; when the Savior comes and receives his ready bride, and all who can be are saved in the various kingdoms of God—celestial, terrestrial, telestial, according to their several capacities and opportunities; when sin and iniquity are driven from the earth, and the spirits that now float in this atmosphere are driven into the place prepared for them; and when the earth is sanctified from the effects of the fall, and baptized, cleansed, and purified by fire, and returns to its paradisiacal state, and has become like a sea of glass, a urim and thummim; when all this is done, and the Savior has presented the earth to his Father, and it is placed in the cluster of the celestial kingdoms, and the Son and all his faithful brethren and sisters have received the welcome plaudit—"Enter ye into the joy of the Lord," and the Savior is crowned, then and not till then, will the Saints receive their everlasting inheritances (Brigham Young, JD, Vol. 17:117).

❏ THE EARTH WILL BE RESURRECTED

And I saw the stars, that they were very great, and that one of them was nearest unto the throne of God; and there were many great ones which were near unto it;

And the Lord said unto me; These are the governing ones; and the name of the great one is Kolob, because it is near unto me, for I am the Lord thy God: I have set this one to govern all those which belong to the same order as that upon which thou standest (Abraham 3:2–3).

. . . This earth will be rolled back into the presence of God, and crowned with celestial glory (*Teachings of the Prophet Joseph Smith,* p. 181).

For all old things shall pass away, and all things shall become new, even the heaven and the earth, and all the fulness thereof, both men and beasts, the fowls of the air, and the fishes of the sea;

And not one hair, neither mote, shall be lost, for it is the workmanship of mine hand (D&C 29:23–25).

Those who are accounted worthy to inherit this earth, when it shall be made heavenly, celestial beings will people the earth with their own offspring, their own sons and their own daughters; and these sons and these daughters which will be born to these immortal beings, will be the same as you and

I were before we took these mortal tabernacles (Orson Pratt, JD, 20:155–56).

And I saw a new heaven and a new earth: for the first heaven and the first earth were passed away; and there was no more sea.

And I John saw the holy city, new Jerusalem, coming down from God out of heaven, prepared as a bride adorned for her husband.

And I heard a great voice out of heaven, saying, Behold, the tabernacle of god is with men, and he will dwell with them, and they shall be his people, and God himself shall be with them, and be their God.

And God shall wipe away all tears from their eyes; and there shall be no more death, neither sorrow, nor crying, neither shall there be any more pain: for the former things are passed away.

And he that sat upon the throne said, Behold, I make all things new (Revelation 20:1–5).

APPENDIX

A Remarkable Vision
(The original spelling and punctuation is retained)

I went to bed at my usual hour half past nine o'clock. I had been reading the Revelations in the French language. My mind was Calm, more so than usual if possible to be so. I Composed myself for sleep but Could not sleep. I felt a strange stupor Come over me and apparently became partially unconscious. Still I was not asleep, nor awake With strange far away dreamy feelings.

The first I recognized was that I was in the Tabernacle at Ogden sitting on the back seat in the Corner for fear they would Call upon me to Preach, which after singing the second time, they did, by Calling me to the stand.

I arose to speak and said I did not Know that I had any thing special to say Except to bear by Testimony to the Truth of the Latter Day work when all at once it seemed as though I was lifted out of myself, and I said "Yes, I have sumthing to say, it is this—some of my brethren present have been asking me what is Coming to pass, what is the wind blowing up. I will answer you right here what is Coming to pass shortly.

I was immediately in Salt Lake City wandering about the streets in all parts of the City and On the door of every house I found a badge of mourning, and I Could not find a house but what was in mourning. I passed by my own house and saw the same sign there, and asked, "Is that me that is dead?" Sumthing gave me answere, "No, you [shall] live through it all."

It seemed strange to me that I saw no person [on] the street in my wandering about through the City. They seemed to be in their houses with their Sick and Dead. I saw no funeral procession, or any thing of that kind, but the City looked very still and quiet as though the people were praying and had Controll of the disease what ever it was.

I then looked in all directions over the Territory, East west North and South, and I found the same mourning in every place throughout the Land. The next I knew I was just this side of Omaha. It seemed as though I was above the Earth, looking down to it as I passed along on my way East and I saw the roads full of people, principally women, with just what they could carry in bundles on their backs traveling to the mountains on foot. And I wondered how they Could get there, with nothing but a small pack upon their backs. It was remarkable to me that there were so few men among them. It did not seem as though the Cars were running. The rails looked rusty, and the road abandoned, And I have no conception how I traveled myself.

As I looked down upon the people I Continued Eastward though Omaha and Council Bluffs which were full of disease, and women every whare. The States of Missouri and Illinois were in turmoil and Strife, Men killing each other, and women joining in the fight, family against family Cutting each other to pieces in the most horrid manner.

The next I saw was Washington, and I found the City a desolation, The White House Empty, the Halls of Congress the same Everything in ruins. The people seemed to have fled from the City and left it to take Care of itself.

I was next in the City of Baltimore and in the square where the Monument of 1812 Stands, in front of St Charles and other Hotels I saw the Dead piled up so high as to fill the square. I saw Mothers cut the throats of their own Children for the sake of their blood, which they drank from their veins, to quench their thirst and then lie down and die. The waters of the Chesapeake and of the City were so stagnant and such a stench arose from them on account of the putrefaction of Dead bodies that the very smell Caused Death and that was singular again i saw no men except they were dead, lying in the streets, and vary few women, and they were Crazy mad, and in a dying condition. Every whare I went I beheld the same all over the city, And it was horrible, beyond description to look at.

I thought this must be the end. But No I was seemingly in Philadelphia, and there every thing was Still. No living soul was to be seen to greet me, and it seemed as though the whole City was without an inhabitant. In arch and Chestnut Street and in face Every whare I went the putrefaction of the Dead bodies Caused such a stench that it was Impossible for any Creature to Exhist alive, nor did I see any living thing in the city.

I next found myself in broad way New York and here it seemed the people had done their best to overcome the disease. But in wandering down Broadway I saw the bodies of beautiful women lying stone dead, and others in a dying Condition on the sidewalk. I saw men Crawl out of the Cellars and rob the dead bodies of the valuables they had on and before they Could return to their coverts in the cellars they themselves would roll over a time or two and die in agony. On some of the back streets I saw Mothers kill their own Children and Eat raw flesh and then in a few minute die themselves. Wherever I went I saw the same scenes of Horror and Desolation rapine and death. No Horses or Carriages, No busses or street Cars, but Death and Destruction every whare.

I then went to the Grand Central park and looking back I saw a fire start and just at that moment a mighty East wind sprang up and Carried the flames west over the City, and it burned untill there was not a single building left Standing whole even down to the wharfs. And the shipping all seemed to be burned and swallowed up in the Common destruction and left Nothing but a Desolation whare the great city was a short time before. The Stench from the bodies that were burning was so great that it Carried a great distance across the Hudson River and bay, and thus spread disease and death wharever the flames penetrated. I Cannot paint in words the Horror that seemed to Encompass me around. It was beyond description or thought of man to Conceive.

I supposed this was the End but I was here given to understand, that the same horror was being enacted all over the Country, North south East and West, that few were left alive. Still there were some.

Immediately after I seemed to be standing on the west band of the Missouri River opposite the City of Independence but I saw no City. I saw the whole States of Missouri & Illinois and part of Iowa were a Complete wilderness with no living human being in them. I then saw a short distance from the river Twelve men dressed in the robes of the Temple Standing in a square or nearly so. I understood it represented the Twelve gates of the New Jerusalem, and they were with hands uplifted Consecrating the ground and laying the Corner Stones. I saw myriads of Angels hovering over them and around about them and also an immense pillar of a Clowd over them and I heard the singing of the most beautif[ul] music the words "Now is established the Kingdom of our God and His Christ, and He shall reign forever and Ever, and the Kingdom shall never be Thrown down for the Saints have overcome." And I saw people Coming from the river and different places a long way off to help build the Temple, and it seemed that the Hosts of the angels also helped to get the material to build the Temple. And I saw some Come who wore their Temple . . . robes to help build the Temple and the City and all the time I saw the great pillar of Cloud hovering over the place.

Instantly I found I was in the Tabernacle at Ogden yet I Could see the building going on and got quite animated in Calling to the people in the tabernacle to listen to the beautiful music that the angels were making. I Called to them to look at the Angels as the House seemed to be full of them and they were saying the same words that I heard Before "Now is the Kingdom of our God Established forever & Ever." And then a voice said "Now shall Come to pass that which was spoken by Isaiah the Prophet that seven women shall take hold of one man, saying . . . (Isaiah 4:). [And in that day seven women shall take hold of one man, saying, We will eat our own bread, and wear our own apparel: only let us be called by thy name, to take away our reproach.]

At this time I seemed to Stagger back from the pulpit & F D Richards and some one else Caught me and prevented me from falling when I requested Brother Richards to apologize to the audience for me because I stoped so abruptly and tell them I had not feinted but was exhausted.

I rolled over in my bed and heard the City Hall Clock strike Twelve (from Wilford Woodruff's Journal, 7:419–23).

BIBLIOGRAPHY

Latter-day Saint Scriptures

The Book of Mormon. (trans.) Joseph Smith. Salt Lake City: The Church of Jesus Christ of Latter-day Saints, 1989.

The Doctrine and Covenants of the Church of Jesus Christ of Latter-day Saints. Salt Lake City: The Church of Jesus Christ of Latter-day Saints, 1989.

The Holy Bible. King James Version. Salt Lake City: The Church of Jesus Christ of Latter-day Saints, 1989.

The Pearl of Great Price. Salt Lake City: The Church of Jesus Christ of Latter-day Saints, 1989.

Other Reference Works

Cowley, Mathias F. *Wilford Woodruff: History of His Life and Labors as Recorded in His Daily Journals*. Salt Lake City: Bookcraft, 1964.

Deseret Evening News. Salt Lake City.

Deseret News. Salt Lake City.

Ensign Magazine. Salt Lake City: Published by the Church of Jesus Christ of Latter-day Saints.

Eusebius, Pamphilus. *Ecclesiastical History*. Trans. C. F. Cruse. New York: Dorset Press. (Eusebius was bishop of Caesarea in Palestine. He lived from about A.D. 260 to 339.)

Improvement Era. Salt Lake City: The Church of Jesus Christ of Latter-day Saints.

Journal of Discourses. 26 vols. Liverpool: F. D. and S. W. Richards, 1854–86.

Juvenile Instructor. The Church of Jesus Christ of Latter-day Saints.

McConkie, Bruce R. *Doctrinal New Testament Commentary.* 2 vols., Salt Lake City: Bookcraft, 1976.

Millennial Star. The Church of Jesus Christ of Latter-day Saints.

Milner, Rev. Joseph. *History of the Church of Christ.* 5 vols. Edinburgh: Peter Brown and Thomas Nelson, 1836.

Mosheim, Dr. J. L. von. *Ecclesiastical History.* 6 vols. 1755. Trans. James Murdoch. London: William Teff and Co., 1764.

Neander, Augustus. *Christian Religion and Church.* Trans. Joseph Torrey. New York: Hurd and Houghton.

Pratt, Parley P. *A Voice of Warning, and Instruction to All People, or an Introduction to the Faith and Doctrine of the Church of Jesus Christ, of Latter Day Saints.* Manchester: W. Shackleton and Son, 1841.

Smith, Joseph, Jr. *History of The Church of Jesus Christ of Latter-day Saints.* Ed. B. H. Roberts. 2d ed., rev. 7 vols. Salt Lake City: Deseret Book, 1978.

Smith, Joseph Fielding. *Doctrines of Salvation.* 3 vols. Salt Lake City: Bookcraft, 1954–56.

Smith, Joseph Fielding. *Essentials in Church History.* 13th ed. Salt Lake City: Deseret News Press, 1950.

Smith, Joseph Fielding. *Signs of the Times.* Salt Lake City: Deseret News Press.

Smith, Joseph Fielding. *The Way to Perfection: Short Discourses on Gospel Themes.* 5th ed. Salt Lake City: Genealogical Society of Utah, 1943.

Smith, Joseph Fielding, comp. *Teachings of the Prophet Joseph Smith.* Salt Lake City: Deseret Book, 1976.

INDEX

G

Gathering
  of elect, 21
  of Gentiles, 40
  of Israel, 21, 49, 85
  of Saints, 37–38
  of ten tribes, 87-91
Gentiles
  armies of, 99
  to assist Jacob, 77-79
  fulness of, 19
  gathered, 40
  remnant of Jacob among, 45
  time of, 93
Germany, 26
Gog and Magog, 131-132
Gospel, 126-127
  of Jesus Christ restored, 13-17
  will spread, 21
Government, overthrown, 43-44

H

Heavens
  signs in, 108–10
  silence in, 110
Holy Land, 50. *See also* Israel, Jerusalem
Hyde, Orson, 26

I

Israel. *See also* Holy Land; Jerusalem; Jews; Judah; Palestine
  captivity of, 85
  gathering of, 20, 49-50, 85
  lost tribes of, 86, 87–89
  shall return, 87
  State of, 51
  ten tribes of, 85–86
  tribes of, 85

who is, 85
Independence, Missouri, 80-81

J

Jackson County, Missouri, 71-76, 82, 95
Jacob
  assisted by Gentiles, 77
  remnant of, 45, 77-79
  shall flourish, 97
Japan, 24
Jerusalem. *See also* New Jerusalem
  dedicated, 50
  Jews will turn to, 49–50, 100
  will be rebuilt, 52-53
Jesus Christ
  all will bend knee to, 128
  coming of, 104, 107, 112, 114
  did not reveal time of coming, 107
  established Church, 1–2
  sign of, 109–10
  will come to Jerusalem temple, 57
  will come to New Jerusalem temple, 81
  will reign, 123
Jews. *See also* Israel
  build up wastelands, 51
  gather to Holy Land, 49
  mission to, 93
Judah. *See also* Israel
  fate of, 86
  will gather, 49-51
Judge
  Apostles will, 129
  Jesus Christ will, 137–38
Judgments, 26, 31, 36-37, 123, 137–39

T

Talmage, James E., 6-10, 17, 87, 89-90
Taylor, John, 44, 76, 79, 83, 117
Telestial hosts, 121
Temple, 40, 41, 102, 130
  in Jerusalem, 21, 49, 50, 52, 57
  in New Jerusalem, 69, 76-78, 80-83, 90, 146
Temple work, during Millennium, 130
Ten tribes of Israel, 87-91, 101
Terrestrial sphere, 31-33, 111
Thrones, will fall, 26
Twelve Apostles, 129

U

United States, 43-44

W

Warnings, first to Gentiles, 120
Wars, 23, 29, 33, 43, 100,
  begin at South Carolina, 23
  city against city, 43
  increasing, 29
  nation against nation, 25
  rumors of, 21, 33, 100
  in United States, 43
Wastelands, built up, 50
Waters
  cursed, 35
  healed, 52
Whitney, Orson F., 67, 111
Wicked
  to be burned, 113, 117
  don't accept gospel, 126-28
  during Millennium, 123, 126-28
  to be swept off earth, 113
Wirthlin, Joseph L., 25

Woodruff, Wilford, 26, 35, 36, 40, 41, 44, 46, 50, 54, 76, 130

Y

Yellow dog, not so much as, 71
Young, Brigham, 26, 29, 36, 45-46, 69, 71, 128-29, 139

Z

Zion
  city of, 39, 75-80,
  Enoch's city called, 115
  Enoch's city caught up to heaven, 115
  Enoch's city to come down, 116-17
  established before return of Ten Tribes, 88-89
  establishment of, 75-80, 83
  kings will come to, 83
  as the Lord's abode, 130
  nations will learn of, 98
  New Jerusalem to be called, 76, 78-79
  as praise of the earth, 79, 83
  redeemed before Christ's return, 95
  righteous will flee to, for safety, 79, 83-84, 99

About the Author

Norma Pyper Mitchell was born and grew up in Salt Lake City, Utah. She graduated from Brigham Young University with a degree in music and teaching certifications in special education. She taught children with learning and behavior problems until her retirement in 1996. Norma has held many positions in the Church at both ward and stake levels and has written and directed several road shows and musical productions. She is currently an accompanist for the Madsen Women's Chorus and the Utah Polynesian Choir and enjoys attending national poetry conventions. She lives in Pleasant Grove, Utah, is the mother of seven children, and serves as an organist in the Mount Timpanogos Utah Temple.